David's Journey

First published in Great Britain as a softback original in 2018

Typeset in Minion Pro

Editing, design, typesetting and publishing by UK Book Publishing

www.ukbookpublishing.com

ISBN: 978-1-912183-54-8

MEMOIRS OF A CHIMNEY SWEEP

THIS BOOK IS DEDICATED
IN MEMORY
of A BEST FRIEND DAVID MILLER
1947 -1968
and
MY SISTER FAY 1945-2005
R.I.P.

Fay...1945--2005.
R.I.P.
Untill we meet again with Gods blessing,on his paradise earth.

I thank my wife Evelyn for printing and organizing all the photos and the artwork for this book.

I would like to thank Pam for her skills in helping me set out the book....p.s, and her patience.

Contents

David's Journey

1965
My Journey with a few funny Moments on the way

Introduction

I have never thought to write of my past events, and stories that have played a part in my life, mainly as I feel that others may have had a more interesting past to write about. I'm sure that's true, but with that in mind, I do not want these writings (or mini book, as I prefer to call it!) to come over as some kind of biography, as it may smack of a me-ism book… something I desperately want to avoid. So one may ask, and rightly so, what then is the purpose of this document or mini book? Well, at my age now, into my late 60s, I really believe that myself and others born around the same time, lived through a very interesting period:

Schooling through the 1950s

Teenage and youth through the '60s

Without wishing to be biased, and of course, I can only talk from a personal point of view, a 1950s childhood was so different from one today, in Britain. And, as for the 1960s, it would touchstone a rocket, taking off, exciting in its journey, as everything was changing so quickly.

Hopefully on this potted journey, I will touch on a little of the social history and mention some history of the local area of Swanley, Kent, where I grew up. Also if I may add, just about all these stories have been locked up in my head for 50-60 years, and I have never spoken about them to my family, or to anybody else. Recently in 2015, I began to think that, maybe, with the year 1965 being 50 years ago, it is a good time to air them, especially on reflection, as I believe that 1965 seemed quite a pivotal year for me.

As I enter old age, now is probably the time to exercise them from my mind. Of course, it's not entirely possible to be completely rid of memories, as they are a part of you; for better or worse, they shape you, as to who you are. In fact, there are many other funny situations and characters left out of the mini book, because there is only so much you can write about without the project becoming a heavy plod, as I really want to keep it all light and flowing, focussing just on a specific period, mainly around and leading up to 1965. It would include schooling 1950s style, boxing, a parachute regiment and becoming one of Jehovah's Witnesses. It depicts the end of one way of life and the start of another…so buckle up and away we go!

Childhood and schooling, 1950s style!

I was born in March 1946 – that's right, I was one of the so called 'baby boomers'! The Second World War had just finished and my dad would remain in the army until the following year, 1947.

What a time! Post-war Britain gave evidence of a war that would remain for at least another 10 years. Locally, there were a few bombed out buildings and many air raid shelters scattered around. Much of London still remained flattened because of the bombing she had sustained. Hitler may have been dead a while, but evidence of his handiwork was everywhere, and rationing would continue up until 1954. As for myself, my life was almost a non-starter! Living in a recently built prefab in 1947, at Lullingstone Avenue, Swanley, and around 18 months old, one day, I found my way out of the garden gate and wobbled along the pathway, and on reaching the road, I then promptly lay down alongside the kerb, along the gutter, and fell asleep! Bad enough, however, it was under the wheels of a parked lorry! In the meantime, my mother decided to search for me, and on finding me, scooped me up, just in time, before the lorry driver jumped into his cab after his late morning cup of tea! When my mother told me the story some years later, I just felt relieved that we lived in a prefab without stairs, as she could have been easily another 10 minutes looking…

Later, around 1949, we moved onto the St Mary's Estate, to Rowan Road, which was about to grow into a massive housing complex over the next 10 years. One tends to forget, or maybe we simply do not realise, just how huge these estates were, with one being built after the other. Sometimes, there were two or three being built simultaneously in Swanley, with the same thing going on all over the country.

This continued for some time, slowing down in the 1970s and '80s. These days, you rarely see large building projects such as the ones that took place back then, except for commercial or industrial buildings, or maybe offices, but never for social housing.

During the 1950s, St Mary's estate became a massive building site! As one site was completed, another one was started. These would all be linked up by road systems and pathways. For young lads, like myself, it was a paradise playground! As soon as the builders knocked off work, us boys would descend on the brand new empty houses! It was like open season! One of our favourite stunts was to climb up the scaffolding and jump off into a pile of sand, again and again! I must just say though, that while we got up to all sorts of mischief, we never thought of vandalising anything or stealing things which didn't belong to us... perhaps a sign of the times...

Building sites today are heavily fortified with fencing, boarding and perhaps a patrolling security guard.

Buildings held a fascination for me from an early age. In 1949, when we moved into Rowan Road, houses were still in the process of being built opposite us. Scaffolding was everywhere, and, as a three-year old, the temptation to climb was just too much! Once again, I escaped through the garden gate, crossed over the road and climbed up the scaffolding ladder, onto the platform. This time though, my dad could see what I was up to, and came over. I can still see him, standing at the bottom of the ladder with his arms stretched out, anticipating whether I was going to leap for it. He then came up the ladder, got hold of me and carried me back down.

As I mentioned earlier, local building sites were a natural playground and held a fascination for me and my pals. You had to watch out for Mr Dockerall though, as he was the night watchman. You kept a look out for him, not because he was nasty; on the contrary, he seemed to be rather a kindly old chap. He lived around 80 yards from my house, and had me earmarked for my wanderings, yet he seemed to respect us kids and acted kindly. If he caught us playing in the empty houses, he would just tell us to move on, and in those days, kids responded very quickly to adult direction, but because we were not afraid of him, we just hid when we sensed him around, resurfacing once the coast was clear… perhaps us kids were better watchmen than he was!

As I tell these stories, it just absolutely amazes me, when I realise the amount of freedom you had as a 1950s child.

Another example would be when I was around 4 years old, sitting in a meadow, across the road from where we lived, looking at buttercups and daisies, all by myself! This piece of land would later become the back gardens of Laburnham Avenue, and Rowan Rd, arranged in back to back style, which is interesting, because 65 years ago, Laburnham Avenue was a continuation of Brook Road, which would follow on up to the railway line. Brook Road started, as it does today, from the A20, opposite Heathfield Terrace, running for half a mile up to the railway line. At the start on the right hand side of Brook Road was a large house, then there was some waste ground, with the same on the left hand side for about 300 yards. Way over to the right was the Crescent Garden estate, which was started in the 1930s and completed in the 1950s. Three hundred yards up Brook Road, on the right, was a footpath, which is now Dale Road. Going up the footpath about 150 yards, was a small holding to the right. Following the footpath a little more, there was a row of small bungalows, then a footpath crossroads. Straight over was Trunks Alley, which came out at Hockenden Lane. To the right of the main crossroad, for about half a mile, the other footpath took you to Birchwood. If you went to the left, however, you passed a large pigsty, with scrubland to the right. On the left was farmland, all owned by Woods Farmers. The footpath carried on through Windmill Wood (we named it Little Woods) and on to Crockenhill. Going back to the footpath, which is now Dale Road, all the area to the left was farmland. If you went up Laburnham Avenue, all that was farmland too. It would encompass Sermon Drive, Bourne Way, Farm Avenue, Lyndon Way and all the roads in that surrounding area. The farmland was a variation of potatoes, peas, cornfields and fruit trees with apples and pears.

The Woods family had been farming the land for many generations up to the 1950s. They owned a farmyard and farm house which was halfway along Brook Road (which is now Laburnham Avenue). There was a driveway leading up to the farm, where the family lived.

Again, a little further along Brook Road, the farmland would end and to the right of it was a large meadow about 300 yards square. To your left was a large field (normally potatoes) which would become the playing fields for Swanley Secondary School from about 1956. With your back to the playing fields, looking down across the meadow, which was once farmland left to fallow – this kind of thing happened all the time, when farmland was sold off to developers – to the right of the meadow was Windmill Wood, a small wood with a footpath which connected up to the Bull of Birchwood.

As mentioned earlier, we called this wood 'Little Woods', as it was about 200 yards square. At the bottom of the meadow was a much larger wood, probably twice the size of Little Woods, so we named it 'Big Woods' (correct name for it was Bourne Wood), with a lovely stream that ran right across the front of the wood.

With my friends, we would spend many hours in Little Woods and as we got older, we would even spend nights in the wood, often by a camp fire. As for Big Woods, we would venture over there from time to time. It was much more foreboding and mysterious. Very few people would wander over there as it always seemed a bit spooky! It was quite an attractive wood with some large trees and nice footpaths. It was very quiet and, as I remember, it was not the sort of place you would want to wander around on your own, although four of us boys made a cabin type camp and all slept in it overnight a few times, but it was spooky!

1944

EVELYN

Mum and Joan
1948.

1946

DAVID

1949

1949..David,Joan,Marion (family friend). out side st mary,s church Swanley.

1950.. David at Nan and Grandad White.

David..age 4, with Smokey the dog. 1950.

Dad,Nan,Aunt Sadie,
and Aunt Pearl.
1947

School, 1950s style

From being a five-year old, I would spend the next six years at Farningham Hill Primary School. The school was around two miles away from where I lived in Rowan Road. This was a fair walk for a five-year old, but even so, in those days, your mother would leave you at the garden gate, not the school gate. You just got on with it, making your way down Rowan Road until you found the footpath (which is now Oliver Road). It led up a hill and to the left was a field which was sometimes potatoes, and sometimes a cornfield. Near the top of the hill was a large sand pit. This was a crater formed when a bomb landed during the war. Further over was a large area of ferns. If you carried on further up the footpath, you met the old part of Oliver Road, which was a continuation of Lime Road. You would then meet the A20, London Road. I do not remember any arranged authority or person to help us to cross over this busy main road. We would meet in small groups and perhaps a kindly mum would see us safely across the road. At this point, I would check to see if the bus was coming over the hill by The Bull of Birchwood, about a quarter of a mile away. Even if it was, I would try and chance it and beat the bus!... To help slow things down there were about four stops on the way to my school, and I had the bus fare, a few pennies, burning a hole in my pocket. I tried to time it so I could run into a sweet shop on the way. More often than not, the bus would go flying past me, perhaps near to the bus garage, which left me a quarter of a mile to run and a five-minute dash before reaching school. The bus travelled through Swanley. This has vastly changed: there was no

Asda and no precinct, as the main road, London Rd, A20, ran straight through to where the precinct is now. There was also a 1930s Art Deco style cinema, The Corona, with a forecourt for a few cars, and one or two electrical shops. Next door, a little further down, was a Catholic church, made of wood. This burnt down in the 1960s. All that ground remained waste until the Post Office was built in the 1970s.

Next to that waste ground was an Art Deco building with a row of shops on the ground floor. The café on the corner was called The Sugar Loaf, next door to that was a bicycle shop and further down was a jeweller's outlet. On the other corner was a haberdashery shop called Betty's. Over the top there was about 6 flats, with flat roofs and a staircase at either end. Further down was the railway line and railway bridge. Where the roundabout is now, there was a set of traffic lights. The footpath would run parallel to the railway line, as it does now, and lead up to Swanley recreation park, or The Rec, as we would call it. Basically, the area has not changed much in 60 years, except the play area has now moved to the other side of the park. Down at the bottom, parallel to St Mary's Road, is the Community Centre, built in the 1950s and rebuilt around the 70s.

Opposite the recreation park, along St. Mary's Road, Swanley School has been in the same spot for 70 years, but was rebuilt in the 1980s. The other part of the secondary school was built at the other end of St Mary's Road in the 1950s, then pulled down and rebuilt 40 years later. Around 15 years after that, it was all pulled down again to make way for a new housing estate.

Returning to being a five-year old again, it always amazes me that, as kids, we always learned how to just get on with it. Now of course, things are so different, and have steadily changed over 60 years, being almost unrecognisable in comparison. For example, I don't remember children being driven to and from school, as they are now, or even parents escorting children to the school gates. Yes of course, it did happen, especially if mums lived just 5 minutes away, but not on the same scale as today. There always seemed to be groups of kids making their way to school, and they did not always live just around the corner. My school, Farningham Hill, was the best part of a two-mile journey for myself and others too.

It was the same school that my mother went to, which I believe is why I ended up going to the same school.

Going home from school was the same journey, but in reverse. I hardly ever caught the bus, or I tried to beat it. I know it took a lot longer as I was notorious for larking about with a few pals, perhaps taking an hour or so to get home!

My Nan and Grandad's house was always a good detour, with a sweet shop 20 yards away, as they lived in the second terraced house at the beginning of the High Street. Nan was always good for sixpence (two and a half pence). A birthday visit would always be a must. Two shillings (ten pence) was the normal going rate. The sweet shop was en route, so any money received was well spent. These school journeys, which were quite normal to myself, would be very hard to explain to children in today's world. For many obvious reasons, they cannot be allowed that same freedom, but I am sure that looking back as I reach old age, it was a far more enriching time and one that I am grateful for, not being fetched and carried everywhere. By way of example, I would like to cite a typical journey of my walk from school. One day, as a little boy of just seven years old, I was coming home from school all on my own. It was Summer 1953, just before Summer Term and this is why I can be so precise with the evidence of the occasion. As I walked through Swanley, I crossed over the railway bridge, turned left and walked up the footpath towards Swanley Recreation Park, then as I got to the Park, I met my Aunt Pearl, coming out of the Secondary School. Pearl was my dad's sister, who was 15, eight years older than me, and was about to leave school at the end of Summer term around July and start work. She had to crouch down, in a concerned way, as any aunt would, saying 'David, will you be alright to get home?' I would have said 'Yes'. This was at about the halfway point of my journey. We then parted and both went to our homes. This is a fairly typical situation of how a seven-year old had to learn to get from 'A' to 'B'. I would not dream of my grandchildren doing the same, but obviously, they were different times. The world was a much different place.

Those days, our playgrounds were all over the place, woods, fields and local countryside near to home. Children and adults would walk everywhere. To have a bike would be like a two wheeled Rolls Royce to us kids and so it was a constant desire to have a bike as soon as possible.

Fay Joan and
David
1949

1952 ..Broadstairs
with Joan and Fay

1951, Mum.. Dad.. David ..Fay ...Joan bus outing,

The Festival of Britain 1951

For a five-year old, it was a very exciting time, when one sunny lovely day in July, my Dad would take me by train to Battersea and visit the Festival of Britain. The colour was spectacular to a five-year old, plus all the sideshows, catwalks, fairground rides etc. It all seemed so very magical.

And then there was LuLu… the dancing doll. Simple, effective, just a cardboard cut-out with metal ringlets in arms, legs and neck. A ringlet in the top of the head which you put cotton thread through and like a puppet, by moving the puppet in an up and down motion, LuLu the puppet appeared to dance! Great Fun! I can still see LuLu… a colourful dancing girl, with short curly hair, costing two and six or half a crown (twelve and a half pence).

Once we got LuLu home, we set her up in a doorway with the thread being pulled through a small metal eye screwed to the top in the middle of the door frame. Us kids were mesmerized by LuLu's dancing, all done on command. Dad would say 'LuLu, stand up' and she would stand; my mum would operate the cotton thread. In operating LuLu, the trick would be for one person, Dad (Tom), to issue commands to LuLu, then Mum (Joan) would operate out of sight, the cotton thread around her finger, moving the doll in an up and down dancing motion. The most fun we had with LuLu was to set up Dad's young brother Maurice. Maurice was 17 years old. A few months later he would be going into the army for his National Service; in fact he signed on as a regular and served 3 years as a PTI (Physical Training Instructor). He was already a boxer, and boxed for the regiment... so he was close to our house on the building site. He was a plastering apprentice and labourer and he would pop in for a cup of tea and a sandwich during his lunchbreak.

On this particular day, during his lunchbreak, the stage was set for him to meet LuLu... and be done up like a kipper! So round he came, all quite innocently. Dad brought him in, sat him down with a sandwich and a cup of tea, and then the fun would start. 'How did it go at the Festival up at Battersea?' enquired Maurice. 'It was great!' replied Tom. 'Me and David had a good day out! We really enjoyed ourselves and there is something we bought back that I'd like to show you. It's LuLu!' … 'LuLu? What's that then?' asked Maurice. 'A lovely dancing doll. It's over there in the doorway, lying down at the moment resting, but if you speak nicely to her, she will do a little dance. Watch this!' replied Dad. 'LuLu… stand up please,' commanded Dad. LuLu instantly stood up! Maurice suddenly lost interest in his sandwich, as LuLu started to dance up and down. He looked at LuLu, then at Dad, then back to LuLu. 'That's amazing! How does she do that? Half a crown? Well, I'm definitely going up to Battersea to get one of those!' said Maurice. After a while and a good laugh, they let Maurice in on the secret.

Recently, I questioned Maurice about the dancing LuLu, all those years ago. I wanted to get my facts straight before I committed them to paper. We had another laugh about it all, especially when I asked how long Dad had kept him in suspense about the secret of how she worked… 'Well,' said Maurice, 'it was before I went back to work, so it saved me half a crown and trip up to Battersea.'

Maurice would serve his three years in the army. Later, he would become one of Jehovah's Witnesses, and is still serving as an elder in Swanley Congregation.

Working on the farm

In the summertime, in order to earn an extra few shillings, our mums would go to the local farm for pea picking, gooseberries, strawberries and sometimes perhaps, apples and pears off the trees. The farmland would later disappear and become Laburnham Avenue, Farm Avenue and Lynden Way. This farm work would be done in the very early 1950s on the farmland, belonging to the Woods Family. While our mums were busy, us boys would be playing around the farm. One day, I decided to investigate the farmyard. I climbed aboard a tractor, as there was no one around. Discovering the diesel tank cap, I unscrewed it and began to fill it up with pebbles and stones! The farmer came out, caught me and gave my mum the sack straight away! Funny though, how sometimes your sins may come back to haunt you, perhaps even years later. This happened to me about 40 years after the incident: I was doing some work at a bungalow in Birchwood for Farmer Woods' daughter. She was probably about 20 years old at the time of the 'tractor' incident and she was a nice looking blonde girl who would drive around the farm in a van, and always have a nice smile... All these years later, when I called at her bungalow, she took one look at me and said, 'You're David aren't you? You were a very naughty boy who got your mum the sack at my dad's farm!' Anyway, a lot of water had run under the bridge by then and I believe I was forgiven. Wounds were healed and we had a good laugh about it all. She told me how much life had changed for them once they had sold the farm, with its hundreds of acres, and then started a new way of life.

Hill Top Farm

As kids during those years, local farms were another terrific kind of playground. If your mums had a problem on one farm, you could just move on to another farm. That's just what my mum did… sacked from one but employed by another, which happened to be Hill Top Farm on the outpost of Swanley. It was more Farningham, or, Farningham Hill really. The red bus, the 21A, took care of the journey. Though it was known as Hill Top Farm, it was also known as Top Farm, which is what we called it. Later on, in modern times, it is now known as Pedham Place… which actually was its original name. Once the day was done, we would hop onto the 21A, to go back through Swanley and home. Actually, the Farm was only perhaps a quarter of a mile away from my Primary School. The farm was well established, and a great place for a little curious boy like me. It was known for its fruit: apples, pears, plums and cherries etc. While Mum and the other mums were busy picking fruit, myself and some of the other boys would be all over the farm like a rash. There was an old army fort and it intrigued the life out of me, so I investigated it as best I could, when no one else was around. I believe it may have housed German POWs 10 years earlier. They worked as enforced labourers, but, certainly an improvement on being sent to the Russian Front. The fort seemed a mysterious collection of buildings with a forecourt. To us kids in the early 1950s, it seemed empty, only housing farmyard equipment, ready as needed to earn its keep. Elsewhere on the farm, there were two, maybe three lookout towers, left over from the Second World War. Again, a natural attraction for 7 and 8-year old boys. The wooden buildings were about 25 feet high and looked like windmills without sails. They were cone-shaped, with windows all around the top, so ideally used as RAF lookout towers. One day, we decided to investigate one of them, and tried the door.

Yes, it opened, straight in front was a stairway, so up we went! Great Fun! After a while, the door opened at the bottom and down below was a young man in RAF uniform, just standing there. He was probably a young squaddie of about 19 years of age, perhaps doing his National Service, but on this day, he was checking up on the lookout towers on the farm. Boy! Did he let us have it! He bawled at us with such bad language, it made the air more blue than his uniform! 1950s children were seldom exposed to that type of language. It was not common at school, in the playground or at home with parents and other adults. They would consciously avoid using bad language in front of children. It is sixty years ago, and I shut it off from my mind, so as not to remember the language said. I would not repeat it even if I could. Running down the stairway, all those years ago, behind the other two boys, I can still hear the last word from "squaddie foul-mouth". As we ran past him and jumped through the doorway, his final goodbyes definitely ended with the word "OFF"!

Another time, three of us felt that we had to flee for our lives! One day we were having a great time playing in a haystack. We had been climbing and jumping all over it, when all of a sudden, from around the side of the stack, stepped a farm worker, all flat cap, braces and waistcoat, with a 12 bore shotgun under his arm. We took one look at him and, like 3 rabbits, took off as fast as our little legs could go! I don't remember him saying a word to us and we certainly didn't want to stick around to find out what he may have wanted to say; however, after a short sprint, I just had to stop to see what he was going to do. As I did, I could see he was not running after us, trying to catch us. The job of scaring us off was done. So I paused and glanced back; he had the 12 bore gun raised in the air, above his head, and he let off a cartridge with a loud bang! Sheer classic... never to be forgotten picture.

Sad now to think that like all the rest of the farmland in and around Swanley, Top Farm (Pedham Place) was to become a massive Golf Course. The whole way of life for farm workers who worked the land is now gone. Such is the blight of so called modern progress. My old Primary School, which was opposite and on the other side of the A20 main road, and built in 1902, would be demolished during the 1970s to make way for an Industrial Estate. More modern progress, it would seem.

The only road system through Swanley before the by-pass was the Old London Road A20, which went straight though Swanley going on towards Farningham. My school was situated at the end of Swanley, close to Farningham Hill. Farningham By-Pass was built in 1926. It's strange to think that in living memory all the traffic would have at one time gone through Swanley and Farningham, known as the London Road. It would have gone past The Lion Hotel, a coaching Inn at Farningham where people dined and rested up or stayed the night. Horses were watered, fed and changed for fresh ones etc., then they carried on the journey, perhaps to Folkestone or Dover.

To return back to my old school, it's 1953 and I'm seven years old. There are around six teachers, a mixed bunch: four females and two male teachers who taught 9-11 year olds. The headmistress was a small, squat woman, Miss Watson, who always seemed to be dressed in dark navy blue, and was headmistress when my mother attended the school. She ruled the school in a very firm, disciplined way, was strict and took no nonsense.

One thing that would fascinate me about her was, that for some reason she seemed to have an enlarged right hand, fat compared to her left hand. Not sure if it was a deformity or some kind of illness incurred, but watch out in her office if she were ever to reach down – that was where she found the cane. It was a 2-foot-long blackboard pointer, fat one end and thin the other, just like her hand I suppose. If you were unfortunate to receive a whack with 'the regulator', it was normally one whack on the palm of each hand. I would receive the cane, fat end, with the fat hand, on a couple of occasions at school. The other female teacher whom I would dread even more than Miss Watson, was Miss Hickson. Like Miss Watson, she was probably around 60 years of age, hence a child old enough to have had their beginnings during the reign of Queen Victoria. That's how I thought of them, as two old Victorian fossils!

I've already described Miss Watson's dress code. Miss Hickson's dress code would be brown all the way down. A spindly spinster, glasses, hair done with a bun, she always seemed to be looking downwards, and would never seem to smile, let alone laugh out loud. Her voice would screech and it all got worse if she came up close to your work desk and let fly at you for some reason. She would screech just talking normal, which would be followed by a haze of spittle as she huffed and puffed and fumed at your poor work.

Of course, in fairness to Miss Hickson, she most probably was a kindly old soul but I'm looking back and seeing myself as a little boy of seven or eight years old. Laughing about these things would only come later on in life, but at the time it made for sleepless nights.

Miss Rogers and the Queen's coronation – 1953

Any fear of Miss Hickson would be balanced out by Miss Rogers, the most wonderful lady teacher a little boy of seven years old could have. I would be a year in her class. She was so lovely. Probably in her early 30s, pretty, with red or auburn hair. She would be my favourite teacher during the 10 years of schooling. Whether or not she had a soft spot for me, I don't know, but I like to think that she did. I'm sure some other children would have felt the same way, but, when addressing me, she would always seem to say, 'David, would you do this, or that' and 'thank you very much, David', but writing this story about my time in her class, there is one incident that might typify Miss Rogers as such a lovely person. It was 1953. The country all over was celebrating the Monarchy, the Coronation and TV, which was making an entry in a big way. All kinds of special activities, fetes, sporting events, street parties and get-togethers were taking place in parks and schools. At my school, us kids would line up in the small playground, dressed in our best school clothes with shiny shoes, to parade before Miss Watson, and us boys, one at a time, with the Union Jack flying, go up to Miss Watson, stand to attention and salute. The girls would curtsey, and each of us received a lovely coronation mug. What a lovely memento to cherish. After over 60 years, I wonder if any of the children still have this cherished possession. I expect there are such ones... however, I believe I broke mine within a week.

1953 CORONATION
YEAR

DAVID AGE 7

Everyone was getting involved with the coronation, including schools, and Miss Rogers asked us kids in the classroom, what we would like to do to celebrate the coronation. The Queen Elizabeth ship had just been built, so she suggested all the kids draw, paint, crayon or whatever, a picture of the Queen Elizabeth ship, and she would pin them on the classroom wall. Well, drawing would always be my favourite lesson anyway, something I would gladly do all day. Later, my schooling would include painting as well as drawing, so to draw the Queen Elizabeth Ship, I would have been well up for the task. My mum had to continue to tell the rest of the story, as I cannot remember all the situation completely. There was an open day for parents around the time and Miss Rogers approached my mum, with a big smile to talk about me, saying 'Mrs White, David has been doing very well; however, I have to just say that recently, the children were tasked to drawing a picture of the Queen Elizabeth ship. David did a lovely picture but I'm afraid he rather spoilt it by blitzing the ship with bullets and bombs from enemy aircraft!' And with that they both had a good laugh about it all… Oh, by the way, it never was… pinned up on the classroom wall.

The point of the story is, if Miss Rogers had decided to really have a go at me in disgust at the nature of the picture, I'm sure I would have remembered it, but it just, I feel, reflects how lovely and kind she was that she chose to laugh it off. On the other hand, I would hear Miss Hickson, from time to time, having a go at kids from her class, screeching away as she whizzed around the room, on her broomstick! Our two classes had a sliding wooden divider, which would slide open for school assemblies or large gatherings, so sometimes, because it was not very soundproof, you could hear the class next door and I would think of one day having to leave the comfort zone of Miss Rogers' class, and spend a year with Miss Hickson. What didn't help the situation was my sister Fay in the year ahead of me. Fay, unlike myself, with my almost zero academic skills, was a brilliant scholar, sheer gold! School work would come naturally to Fay. She always got top marks, whatever the subject, was a grammar school girl who never went to grammar. In those days it could and would happen, especially if it was decided there were insufficient places available at the local grammar schools.

Never mind! Fay became a success at Swanley Secondary School, still getting top marks and being top of the class and eventually becoming Head Girl. She was captain of hockey and netball, with an endless lists of accomplishments. Thank goodness I was a year behind her and not everyone was aware of our family connection. Miss Hickson was though! When I had to do my year of penance, in her class, she never tired of reminding me…normally in this way: 'David White! You're nothing like your sister Fay!' which was said whenever she considered my class work was poor.

Around the age of nine, I would spend the last two years of primary school with two male teachers, starting with Mr Craven-Smith. Out of earshot, us kids would refer to him as 'Craven A', after a well-known cigarette brand of the time. He was OK, tall and balding with a rather posh accent and spoke with a plum; I suppose with a name like Craven-Smith, you would have to… I believe he served his time in the army during the war years and he did keep us kids in order though, with his firm tone of voice. Sometimes, if it was hot and sticky, he would take us on what was known as a nature walk, down a country lane, such as Button Street, opposite Top Farm. Walking from school along the large grass verge in crocodile formation, girls holding hands, something that 1950s boys would never do with each other, we would then walk past the Hop Pole Inn, and after 200 yards, we would do a right turn and walk up the footpath, for a further 200 yards, into Farningham Woods, with all its different footpaths. The teacher would try and translate various nature aspects such as the different kinds of plants, trees, and the real birds and bees... Of course, it was so much fun to escape school for a couple of hours and also it would put a thought in my head about my own personal journey of escape from school, one day soon, which I will come to later.

For now, I would like to return to the start of the term in 1955 and meeting Malcolm Beacock, who would become my best classmate for the remaining two years of primary school. Malcolm had just moved into the area at the bottom of Leechcroft and we would sit together in class.

On two famous occasions, Leechcroft Avenue was completely flooded. Because Malcolm's house was raised a little higher, it escaped the worst of the flooding. This was the mid-1950s, and a period of exceptional torrential rain that flooded down from the fields and railway bank. Later, drainage was improved so it would never happen again. Certain families had to be evacuated from their homes and could not return for many months. Malcolm's dad owned a garage in Bexley, with the name 'Beacock's Garage', which remained there for many years. Both parents claimed their 15 minutes of fame when they entered TV on the Hughie Green Show 'Double Your Money' in 1956. At school for the last two years, we became good mates, not always good for each other, rather, a little naughty at times. We also were very different in every way; for example, physically, Malcolm was tall, taller than me… why not? Everyone else was! He wore spectacles… Unlike myself he was not into any type of sports or exercise, football and just generally running about, whereas I would get on people's nerves with my dashing up and down, especially when fighting (normally play fighting), but sometimes it was real fisticuffs, if I thought that someone wanted to take advantage of me because of my size! I believe boys of the 1950s had to be a bit more streetwise than kids today, because of their freedom of movement. We had to create our own code of behaviour with each other in the area we lived and of course the playground and playing field at school. The norm was often the adults would trust the children to try and not give the family a bad name.

Malcolm and I would become good pals and looking back he seemed to remind me of a mini Sergeant Bilko, from the American comedy series…during the 1950s, Bilko was played by Phil Silvers, the comedy actor… I had a weakness for the giggles and Malcolm would play on that. He knew he could put me under the classroom desk with an attack of the giggles… He never got the giggles himself – he would somehow keep in check, calm, even look a bit serious…knowing that it would all make my giggles even worse... but it must be said that what he lacked in physical status, he made up with the gift of the gab.

Costa Del Leysdown… and young parents can be embarrassing….

I was not intending to include Leysdown into the book; it would seem not all things you became involved with are recorded and aired later. You do not think that ordinary things of life would be of interest. Yet as decades go by often people become more and more interested in how people lived their lives, the entertainment of the time, homes lived in, fashion of the furniture…fashion of clothes worn, and of course the music…etc. etc.… And how it has all changed over the recent decades…

With all that in mind perhaps I will spend a little time talking about Leysdown, and a funny story my sisters would not be aware of, built around two photographs, involving our mum and dad...

Leysdown, the little seaside town, a jewel in the Kentish garden, on a mile length of sun drenched piece of coast at the far end of the Isle of Sheppey overlooking the English Riviera…or better known as the River Thames, gateway to the open sea, over to the left the North Sea, to the right the English Channel. If you keep bearing to the right you pass the coastline of Herne Bay, Whitstable, Margate…more jewels in the Kent coastline. From Leysdown if you look across the sea bay to the other side would be Southend, the Essex coastline. On a clear night, you could see Southend's twinkling lights. Along the coastline of Essex, Southend would be the main seaside town for all London. Easy to access. A serious town and a lot going for it like another Bournemouth down on the south coast. As a driver, you would need your wits about you with its many road systems ...in, through and around, and then of course the parking… never normally where you would love to park ...close to everything and overlooking the sea.

All that said, Southend is probably a lovely place to live...Leysdown was more a small playground in comparison, mainly attracting south Londoners, down the A2...and around a 50-mile journey; once you crossed the old wooden clickety clung Bridge onto the Isle of Sheppey you would then turn right onto Leysdown less than 10 miles away…You're unlikely to lose yourself on the island – the road into Leysdown is the same one back out…Since the 1950s the area has changed very little with regard to modernisation, accept where it's been of benefit such as the beach and having a blue flag rating; it is highly recommended …To a boy in the 1950s it seemed a minefield full of rocks and seaweed below the surface ...however, it was a haven for collecting cockles and wrinkles once the tide was out…

As an eight-year-old I would be the first in the family to test the waters of Leysdown. During September 1954 we moved into Lime Road, Swanley. It was a Saturday, the day of the move, and a family friend asked if I could go on holiday with them and their only son Phillip, who was quite a good pal. I felt very excited being allowed to go. So, we spent a week at Leysdown in a chalet. I must have behaved myself as they asked if I could go with them again the following year 1955… this time we spent the week in a caravan.

During 1956 Mum and Dad decided to give Leysdown a try for themselves ...It would be our first main holiday. They would hire a chalet from a local lady with the unforgettable name, Mrs Chittey.

From then on, they were smitten with Leysdown, and soon after, over a period of some 30 odd years, bought into around three chalets and eventually a brick built apartment in a block of flats close to Leysdown centre.

Looking back on the two photographs takes me right back to that first holiday at Leysdown, staying in our chalet...and a couple of funny moments to share...One of the days I somehow convinced Mum and Dad I would be quite safe to go to the beach and play by myself in the sea with an inflated inner tube...I believe they were a little doubtful, but as already mentioned before... 1950s post-war children were used to having that bit more freedom of movement...so with towel and trunks under arm, Inner tube across shoulder, I was soon gone... However, after a short time they came down to the beach with Pearl in the pram, leaving Fay to look after Joan in the chalet...I was having a great time on my own in the surf with my new-found friend, the inflated inner tube. Mum and Dad were just relieved to find me among the people on the beach and not floating off across to Southend on the inner tube ...Having located and called me away from the sea, they then needed me to quickly change so as to return to Fay and Joan on their own in the chalet...but not before two very embarrassing moments...that I have never forgotten.

Dad kindly held up the towel for me to take down my trunks and pull up my pants. However, at the halfway stage, and before I could complete the operation, he decided it would be hilariously funny to whip away the towel like a Spanish matador. Leaving me standing starkers in the middle of the beach...I felt mortified with embarrassment...and more would follow on the way back to the chalet with the pram...for this I will refer to the two photos...we are walking along a wide Broadway... a rough unmade road to accommodate slow moving traffic or groups of people just walking along as it would connect up to Leysdown High Street... likewise we are doing the same to reach the chalet on the holiday site... then suddenly in a mad moment Dad took off like Norman Wisdom on steroids running backwards and forwards across the Broadway, giving it large to groups of people walking along...then he laid on the grass verge, pretending to take photos at different angles in a sort of David Bailey way... Looking back some 60 odd years ago I know now it was an act for my mum's benefit...He could always make her laugh and get the giggles. As can be seen, in the photo, her pushing the pram... myself. A look of surprise and shock... even now I can still remember the embarrassment and what I thought…looking at my dad showing off… The other photo completes the story… myself pushing the pram… Mum taking the picture, I just love the photo… Only recently I have just seen it for the first time, and boy how all the memories come flooding back ...but it did make me laugh…to see the photo, remember it as a 10-year-old and how one felt and then see it now as one reaches old age…and of course so see the funny side… Perhaps I could explain…in the photo Dad looks like the cat who has just found and had all the cream…if you now look at my little 10-year-old face it's looking away from the camera in a complete look of embarrassment…

Well it did happen… twice… within the hour…

David & Mum
Leysdown 1956.

David & Dad
1956 Leysdown.

Meeting my best friend David Miller

September 1954, we moved from Rowan Road to Lime Road. It was up and around the corner, about 600 yards. The first person I saw was my future best pal, who was standing by his garden gate. I will always remember him, standing outside, next door to where we were moving in. He was seven and I was eight years old at the time, and this friendship would continue right through our teenage years and into our early 20s. We were like close brothers and all that kept us apart was that he went to a different primary school and his sport became rugby while I went into boxing. Later he would eventually become a qualified plumber after serving his apprenticeship with the local council. David eventually changed from working on the tools to a good office job, to do with the plumbing industry. He travelled up and down to London and changed from wearing a boiler suit, to a smart office suit. Dave Miller had a lovely family living next door. His parents were about 10 years older than mine. Daisy was Mum, hardworking type, who worked part-time in a local nursery or farm. Her husband Arthur, who was very placid and obliging, would work as a painter and decorator on the local council. He served in the 8th Army during the war years. I believe he was a driver. There were two other sons, Keith, the eldest and Melvyn. David was the youngest. Sadly, both Arthur and Daisy passed on long ago. Eventually, during the late 1950s, they moved into a new council house in a lovely spot, which was the very end house in Lyndon Way, directly next door to Little Woods, which for us boys was a super location as young boys and going into our teenage years we would enjoy years of fun, which I will talk about later.

Going back to my mate Malcolm, we were an unlikely couple of classmates, but because of our differences, we seemed to gel. His gift of the gab was put to good use one summer's day in 1956. We decided to escape school for the afternoon.

I would feign feeling sick and he would escort me safely home. I can still picture the scene: head down, my left arm holding up the school building at a precise 30-degree angle while rubbing my tummy with my right hand, and all this taking place 20 feet from the steps onto the veranda where Malcolm would approach one of the male teachers, Mr Craven-Smith. I carefully positioned myself near enough to hear what was being said, but far enough away to avoid being asked any awkward questions. Up to the plate steps Malcolm, as he then speaks to the teacher: 'Please, Sir, David White has come over feeling very sick. Shall I escort him safely home?' Without hesitation, the teacher gave his consent: 'OK then, off you go'…and we did! The escape was on!

Our plan, once outside the school gate, was to head for Farningham Woods for the afternoon, but first of all, we had to get through the school gate at a steady pace, not too hasty as to raise suspicion. Turn right as if going through to Swanley and my home. At the 200-yard point, turning right onto Beachenlea Lane, so off we went. Suddenly, my tummy felt much better and so our pace quickened.

1947, just before I I went there. Farningham .Hill. School.
heamistresss Miss Watson on left andl
lovely Miss Rogers is on the right.

Parkwood convalscent Home and Entrance.

After a quarter of a mile along Beachenlea Lane was the entry to Parkwood Hospital, a large, beautiful, late Victorian building on beautiful grounds that was looked after by a team of gardeners. It was used for soldiers in both world wars.

We walked through the hospital grounds to the farmland and footpaths beyond. The hospital was on a hill and the footpaths would take us down to Button Street, coming out near the Hop Pole Inn. We crossed over the road, and close by was a footpath which took us up to Farningham Woods, and there we walked around for a while and to visit the pond in the middle of the wood was a must.

The pond is still there today, with tadpoles, newts, dragonflies hovering around, and frogs. After about two hours of wandering around, we decided to call it a day and go off to our homes, arriving back home at the normal time, so as not to arouse suspicion.

I am sure that a younger generation reading this would find it hard to believe that two 10-year old boys could just walk out of school in the middle of the day. They were certainly different times. There were no such things as mobile phones...hardly anyone had a landline! Communication was not always possible. Cars were thin on the ground. Teachers might have lived local to the school, walked, biked or caught a bus. It would seem that teachers had more power to make decisions, knowing that usually parents would back them up and trust them. There was no bureaucratic form filling of any kind and endless lists of do's and don'ts etc. Common sense was the virtue of the day.

School – the following day

Malcolm and I were somewhat apprehensive back at school next day as to … unwelcome reception from any teacher; however, there were no questions asked. Life would go on. So chuffed were we with our success, we thought we would pull off the same stunt two weeks later. The set up was the same as before, same time after dinner, holding up the same school building with my left hand and rubbing my tummy with my right hand. The scene was set ready for the teacher's entry. Again up steps Malcolm to the plate but this time, it's Mr May. 'Please, Sir, David White is sick. Shall I escort him home safely?' Without much hesitation, Mr May played his part rather well. 'OK, off you go,' he said. Well, the Swiss Watch once again, was certainly ticking, and slowly to start with, out we went through the school gate, but this time we headed north, toward my home and beyond where I lived. We would make our way to and through Windmill Woods, commonly called Little Woods and out the other side, to rest up in a farmworker's corrugated tin hut. It was really a shelter for farmworkers that was many years old, even then, in the mid-1950s, but I had earmarked this hut as a ready-made camp from previous campaigns. After some time and putting the world to rights, us two ten year olds decided to call it a day, so that we could arrive back at our homes at the normal respectful time, around 4.30pm.

However, we found it not so easy the next day, back at school. We got the message 'Would Malcolm Beacock and David White report to Miss Watson's office before going into the classroom'. It was then I said

FARNINGHAM HILL SCHOOL

My Primary school
1950.s

to Malcolm, 'If it looks like we're gonna get it (the cane), here's what we do: You don't feel it if you rub soap all over your hands'. So, quickly, we nipped into the toilets and coated our hands all over with carbolic soap and went off to face the music at the Headmistress's office.

We knocked and were told to come in. 'Well,' she said, 'what's going on with you two?' Our eyes glanced at her, then her fat hand, and then the bottom drawer of desk, then back to the fossil again. 'Have you anything to say for yourselves?' Malcolm suddenly, with perfect timing, said, 'Well, Miss, I took David home, but his mum was out. He was not well so I thought it best that I stay with him. He had no key to get indoors and it was 3.30 when she came home and I thought it was too late to come back into school.' For a moment Miss Watson seemed to soften a little, and I lost interest as to whether the fat hand was reaching down to the bottom drawer of her desk. She looked at us both and said, 'Malcolm, you acted very responsibly by staying with David until his mother returned home,' then she held out her hand and shook both of our soapy hands, saying 'Now run along quickly to your class'. Later, we would laugh our heads off, at the thought of her shaking our soapy hands!

Miss Watson and the gramophone

Miss Watson's pride and joy was a gramophone resplendent with a wind up handle on the side! It was a cabinet on wheels, three feet high, made of beech, varnished and shiny. It would be her weapon of choice. Housed and positioned by her office with easy access to launch through the doorway of the two classrooms which were adjacent each side of her office. It was used whenever bad weather kicked in or if Mr May or Craven-Smith were not around, and Miss Watson had to hold the fort. Along with her, often came the wind up gramophone player, with a record that always seemed to be Peter and The Wolf. Most of us kids would hate it when the classroom door would crash open, followed by the cabinet on wheels. The handle would spin and Peter and The Wolf would sing! I don't know about the other kids, but as I remember, my head would drop down on the desk until it was all over with. To set a bigger picture even more so, it may help to remember the scene of the times around the mid-1950s, where the music taste was drastically changing. Bill Haley and the Comets hit the music scene with the hit song Rock around the Clock, which us kids loved, and could not stop mimicking 'see you later alligator' 'in a while crocodile!' We had some fun with that one… (at our school we would sing 'see you later alligator in a whale crocodile') … Soon our time at primary school would be up, but hopefully Malcolm and I would make amends for our lack of success in the academic stakes.

As ten year olds, the class was invited to do some kind of a model building construction, made out of empty match boxes. It would become our pride and joy. The class were to pick the building of choice, working in pairs. The teacher made some suggestions, but left it to us to decide. The suggestions were perhaps a farmhouse, a school, shop, cinema or pre-fab? Yes, I did say pre-fab. We wanted to be different, original, so that's what me and Malcolm decided.

After all, I had spent the first three years of my life in a pre-fab, so I would know something about them. I reckoned that if a pre-fab was put up in two or three days, then we should be able to knock out a model in two or three hours, with some time to spare! A week later, on the chosen day, the class bought in all their empty matchboxes and glue. In our case, we also bought along the roof (a piece of hardboard about 12 x 18 inches), plus another larger piece of hardboard for the ground, and to take care of the garden area, gates, walls and hedges etc. Of course we had to consider window space and doorways so doors could be hung. The pre-fab was swiftly built but I don't remember windows or any doors being hung, let alone a garden gate and hedges. Well what do you expect in two or three hours?! Somehow, I got the honour of proudly carrying our pre-fab home. Why I was to receive this coveted prize of taking it home first instead of Malcolm, I do not know. I would not have won an argument with him over it. On arriving home with my proud work of art, my dad fell about the front room with laughter! I couldn't, at the time, understand that! Though not destined to be the next Christopher Wren, I learned quickly that beauty is in the eye of the beholder, or in this case, the Master Builder! Two weeks later, there was a knock on the front door. My father opened it and there was Malcolm standing there, and he said… 'I've come for the pre-fab. It's my turn to have it.' Once the door was shut, again, my dad fell about the room with more laughter and for years he would tell the story of the pre-fab and seeing Malcolm standing at the door and saying 'I've come to collect the pre-fab. It's my turn to have it!' I know, looking back, that my dad was not being cruel; he was not that way. If he was, and laughter was inappropriate, I would have looked back with hurt feelings. Instead, I realise how funny it probably looked, a small model pre-fab building, the only one ever that looked 'bombed out' without being bombed!

Soon primary school would end, 1957 to be precise, and the rest of my education of 4 years would be spent at Swanley Secondary School, as I failed university…it was their loss I suppose. It would also mean the end of my classroom friendship with Malcolm, as at Secondary School, we were in different classes and moved in different circles. Looking back, I believe that Malcolm was a one-person friend, although I'm sure he mixed well, but we no longer sought to continue our friendship. But friends never seemed lacking on my part, I had many, although you always had your close group of friends; in my case I had 3 main friends: Dave Miller, Les Parker, who was also my other best friend, and Rowley Nicholson. We went through our school and teenage years together and into our early 20s… There are a few funny stories for another time. We would ride our motorbikes for two or three years and had camping holidays together and I would spend nearly two years working on the Forestry Commission with Les and Rowley, which also was often great with some funny times.

As a unit of four, we all felt bullet-proof.

Swanley School rather overwhelmed me. A thousand kids all in all, although of course it had to be divided – 11 and 12 year olds at St Mary's School and 13-15 year olds at Cherry Avenue – it was the size that overwhelmed me. It felt like you were going from a small friendly village (primary school) where everyone knew each other, to a large unfriendly town (secondary school). What did not help, my sister Fay, one year ahead of me, was already making her mark. She would end up in top class and top girl in the class. Always finishing around top in her class exams, becoming a prefect and eventually Head Girl, captain of netball, hockey and so on. Teachers would remember Fay for years afterwards. I would leave no mark. To start with, I was not academic… however…

Boxing

There were so many boys good at sport, athletics and especially football, it would make you feel ordinary and unexceptional. But once I found boxing, a sport I could excel at, around 12 years of age, by the time I was 13, I was making my mark. Not because I needed to do that, it just happened. I would have boxed anyway. It would become quite natural to me. I was in Dartford boxing club. I boxed for the Army Cadets and won my first championship which was Kent Army Cadets Title, but could not go on, because I was too young. I felt very gutted about that, not being able to carry on and try to win the National Cadets title, but from then on I became completely focussed on boxing. I boxed at school. It was part of the National Curriculum. I boxed for the school in the Kent Championships. The boxing club arranged many fights and at 16, got us boys to box in the Sea Cadets to win a National Sea Cadets Title. Any schoolboy that liked boxing would dream about being the National Schoolboy Champion for his weight and age, but it was very difficult, as all schools did boxing, being a part of the National Curriculum. To be a schoolboy champion would be like boxing in the Olympics for kids. With so many boys entering, it would be very difficult. One year I reached the dizzy heights of the Kent Championships. In the course of my time as a boxer, I would box three former schoolboy champions, as I remember, and I was successful against two of them, but one proved evasive and eluded me. That was a boy named Danny Mogford from West Ham, the East End of London.

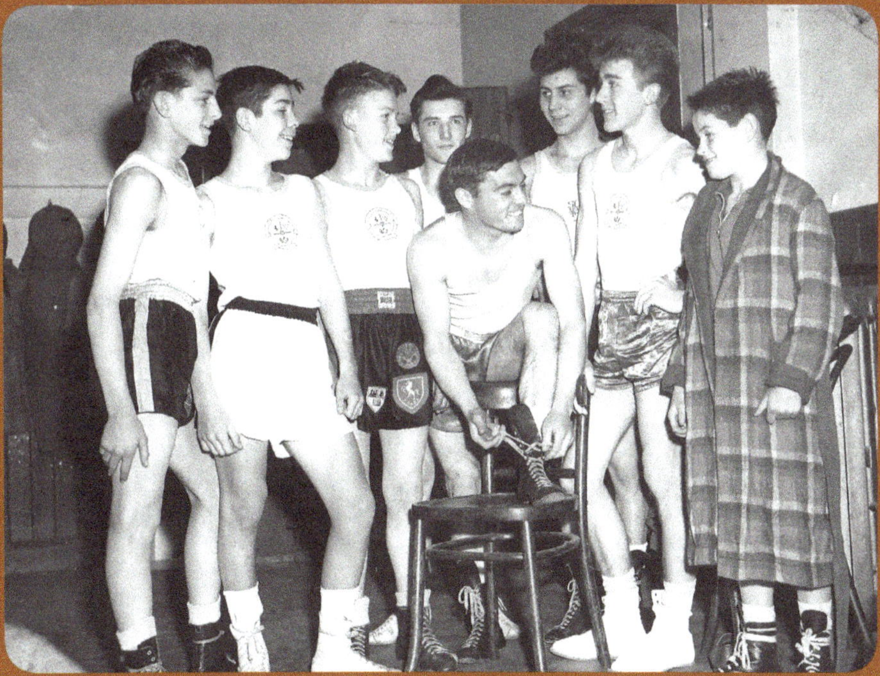

BEFORE THE BOXING TOURNAMENT
LEFT. PAT MANNING.ROGER WENBAN.DEREK ELLIS.
MICHAEL DIXIE,RICHARD WENBAN. BRIAN PACKER. DAVID WHITE,
AND NORMAN STANTON LACING UP HIS BOOTS.

1962...I was no sailor, I only joined for the boxing

Being hammerred at west ham by Danny Mogford,but then he was considered the best in the country..his dad sent a nice letter & shirt as a present of appreciation, see letter over the page.

105, Goldsmith Ave
London: E.12.
24 - 4 - 61

Mr and Mrs. Baker

Dear Sir.

Would you be so kind as to give to D White, this shirt, we hope it fits.

It was very kind of you all to come at such a short notice.

Young White is a very hard boy and with more contests, should be hard to beat, he's a nice kid not afraid who he meets.

And Best Regards
F.C Mogford

They brought him over so as to box me when we were both 14 on a senior boxing show at Dartford. It was considered a great honour to box on a senior show. Danny was so fast and accurate, he swarmed all over me like a butcher's dog. The first round he won easily. In the second round, we were evens, but by the last round, he was punching himself out. I even had to tell him to stop holding onto me. I won the third round and if it had gone into a 4th round, I know I would have won the fight, but Danny won the first round more than I won the third, so he got the decision.

I would meet him again a few months later. By then we were both 15 years old. After that, my Club got a call from West Ham Club to ask if we could oblige them by boxing each other on a show, at West Ham, but it was the very next day. The season was almost finished and I was in no way ready for him, but I obliged. The club secretary picked me up and drove us over, but this time I lost just about every round, and no arguments, but then Danny was London Schools Champion and was reckoned to be the best in the country for his weight and age. Around a week later, we received a very nice letter from Danny Mogford's father, and a shirt, as a present of appreciation. The letter, which I have still got by the way, said I was a hard boxer to beat and that in time I would be a very difficult opponent. As senior boxers, Danny and I came close to boxing almost twice again, but because of circumstances, it never happened. (Another story!) Danny would win the London Featherweight Division in the 1960s. At 16 I would enter Junior boxing, just a year before becoming a senior boxer. In 1962, I was representing the Sea Cadets at Aldershot. It was a competition that involved the winning cadets from the Army, Navy and Air Force, and also the winner of the regular Army Navy and Air Force Juniors. The four winners meet up, and I would be boxing a young Army champion in the morning… When I climbed into the ring, I couldn't believe how tall he was! I was probably only about five feet three inches and only came up to his shoulder, so he would have been about five feet nine or ten inches. Even so, it was quite a scrap and I managed to win. Though I wouldn't have been surprised if I'd lost as it was so close. Unlike the final in the evening I had against the Army Cadet Champion, which I thought was a slightly easier fight, and yet I lost the decision. If I had got that decision, I would have gone onto The Royal Albert Hall for the National Junior Championships, two weeks later.

BOXING TRAINER
& FRIEND,
NORMAN STANTON, 1966

Parachute regiment

Over the next few years, I stayed with my group of pals and my boxing. The one thing I missed out on doing, though, was National Service. I did not want to commit to the regular Army. It was a time when National Service had finished and most lads were glad not to have to do it. The taste of being a paratrooper and wearing the famous red beret, was something I would have liked to have done, especially in National Service. Because you had no say, you joined up for two or three years perhaps. A couple of years in the parachute regiment is something I would have loved to have done. In 1964, when I was 18, I learned about the 10th Parachute Regiment, an Army reservist regiment, stationed at White City, London.

During the 1960s, it was known as 'Ten Para', one of the parachute battalions that served at the battle of Arnhem, Holland, during the Second World War, made famous by the film 'A Bridge Too Far'.

While being interviewed, they asked about my interests. I told them that I was a boxer; they liked that and wanted me on the boxing team.

After I signed up, a short while later, I met up with my best pal Dave Miller. I was in such a rush to join, I didn't think to tell any of my mates that I was joining the regiment, in fact, it all came about when I was watching a promotional film on TV about the 10th parachute regiment. I remember that I was so impatient to join up straight away. Two or three weeks later, I was talking to my mate David and I noticed how interested he was in what I was doing and that he was keen to join. He did, but it had to be in the next group of recruits, behind my group. Even so, we would arrange to do our parachute training together.

You meet a lot of characters in the army and while I was being interviewed, another young chap being interviewed like myself named Frank Eagon, was talking to an officer, who was taking notes. He was saying he was 23, five years older than myself. I'll always remember Frank. He later teamed up with John Watson, who was 22 years old. John joined at the same time. They became good friends and we would all do our para-troop training for a few months together. Both Frank and John were proper South London boys, very funny, wisecracking all the time. John had a dark complexion and was about 5ft 10". Frank, though, was an enigma, a puzzle to me. He stood probably around six foot, handsome, with blonde cropped hair. He had a very relaxed manner about him, spoke softly and had a smiley face. Looking back he looked and reminded me a little of the actor Michael Caine, with a dash of Frank Spencer thrown in (this was long before the comedy show with Frank Spencer was being broadcast), especially the way he would wear his red beret and camouflaged smock jacket. Normally, you would wear a red belt around the waist, over the smock jacket, not Frank though… I don't remember him normally bothering to wear a belt. His smock jacket just hung down and the way he walked, or supposedly marched, was also very funny. It was done with a swagger, but not in a cocky way. He would kind of roll his shoulders and clench his fists as he marched along. He was just so funny, clever with a slow wit behind it all. I'm sure he only ever got away with it, because you felt behind it all was this intelligent mind at work. He certainly seemed to have the right answers at the right time. I'm sure that, generally, sergeants and officers found him so likeable and funny, the same as everybody else, so he just seemed to get away with it. He was just an unusual character. Like myself, both Frank and John were not career soldiers. They probably missed doing National Service by a whisker. We all would join for two or three years, have some fun and then move on with our lives.

Our Para troop training was spent between headquarters at White City and travelling to Aldershot. All told, to start with, there were about 80 lads at the same time, on this training.

We would meet up and learn how to wear uniforms, clean boots, march and go on manoeuvres overnight around Salisbury and Aldershot. We also spent time on the rifle ranch with SLR rifles. The paratroopers' close up weapon was the STEN gun, which I liked most of all.

The months seemed to go very quickly and finally we all had to be assessed and pass tests to see who was capable... This was all done mainly at Aldershot. It meant a lot of running around. We split up into teams, racing each other, carrying telegraph poles, learning to work together as a team, helping each other around the course. Climbing and running about over scaffolding, sometimes quite high. One obstacle was 60 feet high and you had to straddle across two scaffold poles, three feet apart... arms outstretched – all this was testing how we could handle heights. The last thing was to clean ourselves up after all the mud, muck and bullets and then, with nice clean uniforms and polished boots, we assembled on the parade ground for the passing out ceremony. Out of around 80 lads, 20 completed the whole course over a few months. We were then told to assemble, tallest to the left, shortest to the right. We spent a couple of minutes jostling and elbowing each other for the height difference, all the time I realised that I was going further and further down to the right. Nobody wanted to be the shortest, including myself… Finally, the decision was taken away from me and I ended up as the last one, furthest on the right, considered the shortest, although I still believe that I was a good ¼ inch taller than the boy next to me. Fractions are so important at 5ft 5" and when you are 18. All of us lads were young, fit and ready for the next stage, the parachute training. I would wait till around the end of October, for my best pal, Dave Miller, so that we could go together. Like me, David passed his training. I knew he would. He was like myself, into sport and a very active rugby player.

Just before we went to the parachute training, I remember Frank Eagon and Johnnie Watson had just been to parachute training school at Abingdon, Oxfordshire. When they had completed the course, we met them at White City headquarters. They looked over at me and reassured me that the training was nothing to worry about. It would be alright. Piece of cake. You'll love it! So come the end of October 1964, my pal Dave and myself in our Army uniforms and red berets, boarded the train for Abingdon for a two week parachute course.

Monday, we all assembled as a group in a large aircraft hangar, full of swinging harnesses and different apparatus. The floor was covered in coconut mats and a mock up aeroplane fuselage. Everything you need compliant with parachute training. There were around 8 RAF instructors, so we were split into groups of 10, and away we went. It was a very intense course… around 8am in the morning until about 5pm. The evenings were spent in the NAAFI. We would spend the whole week training, which was so well drummed into you. A paratrooper has to learn the correct procedure of putting on a parachute. When you stand up in a plane, you have to check each other's parachute, harness and webbing, as you're getting ready to jump, just before the green light comes on. When you jump, for about 5 seconds, you feel like a little rag doll; as the chute opens, it feels like you are being pulled back up in the air. Once you've checked that the chute is opened and it's functioning ok, you only have about 1 minute until you're on the ground! You check if you're drifting to the left, right, forward or back. The chute acts like a sail, so you learn to counteract that action by pulling down on your rigging. If you're going back, you pull down the front rigging and if you're going to your left, you pull down on the right etc.

This is so important, because in the last 100 feet, the ground comes rushing up towards you like an express train, and then it's a mighty crash into the ground. This is when you must remember the drill: keep your legs together, not too stiff, elbows tucked in and the trick is to hit the ground in a kind of roll, to dissipate the energy by rolling into a ball. The strict training can save you from serious injury, broken legs or arms or sometimes just bruising… Some of it is inevitable. The last two jumps from the aircraft are with two containers strapped to your legs, which have to be jettisoned at the right time. They are joined to your webbing by a 15-foot cord. It's quite a lot to remember in one minute. Natural inclination is that once you feel the relief of looking up and seeing your parachute open, you relax and want to enjoy the ride down, but you mustn't do that. It could be a big mistake.

Balloon jumps are completely different, probably more nerve wracking. Going up in a balloon and jumping from 800 feet.

You could not say that the aircraft was a relaxing atmosphere but there is so much noise and commotion, that you felt part of it all and it's all very exciting. My third aircraft jump, I was told I was first of a stick of eight jumpers... Each side of the aircraft there would be eight jumping, but altogether there would be 32 jumpers. The aircraft would exit 8 from each side and then return and exit another eight from each side. As I stood up, and the red light was on, we quickly hooked up our static line onto a sliding cable and did a quick check of our chutes and also checked the man next to us. By then, the door was slid back, a rush of wind and we are clipping along, probably around 200 miles per hour at 1,000 feet. I am standing in the doorway for perhaps two minutes and it was all very exciting when you're looking down at green fields and hedgerows, waiting for the green light to come on and a friendly nudge on my shoulder from the dispatcher and then it's away we GO, GO, GO!

1964...Abingdon,gettingready to jump from hastings aircraft.

1965
10.Para..Regiment.

A petrified paratrooper

It's quite normal to perhaps wonder or ask if it's nerve wracking to do all that. We are all different and I'm sure we all handle things differently. Some may not handle it at all. There's nothing wrong with that or to be ashamed of. It would seem some would-be paratroopers are more scared than others. I was probably average, but the very next day, I witnessed a petrified jumper sitting right next to me. The following day was the same set up, eight to jump each side, the plane to bank, return and unload another eight each side. This time I was last to jump of a stick of eight. As I went to stand up and get ready, the lad sitting next to me caught my eye. He was sitting down and would be in the next stick of eight to jump in around 10 minutes. He looked absolutely terrified. It's a look I will never forget. His face was wringing wet with sweat, and his eyes bulging in their sockets. For a brief moment it shocked me and I immediately felt sorry for him, but at the same time, I had to ignore him as I was of course under orders to carry out the normal routine equipment and check procedure, which I did. That look though would not leave me. Of course everything was happening very quickly. I'm holding onto the static line, ready for the green light, and I just had to have one last look at that wet flannel of a face. As I did, I leaned over, held out my hand, rubbed his shoulder and called out 'don't worry, you'll be OK', then the green light is on and it's go, go go.

It's funny to remember all this from 50 odd years ago. Strange now. I'm sure that anyone reading this might question what happened to that young chap. I like to think that when it was his turn, he did the jump and finished his parachute course; however, at 18, you don't think that far, you live in the moment whatever it is. It's only going into old age that sentimentality crashes in and you wonder... now, what happened to him.

Once the course was completed another parade to receive our parachute wings sewn on as a shoulder badge.

Job now complete and fully enrolled in the Ten Para regiment. As soon as we got back from parachute school, Frankie Eagon was the first to come over to congratulate us, and with a big grin on his face, asked us how we had got on. So we told him what a great unforgettable time it was. Then he remembered what he'd said to us and then said, 'Well I know I told you it was a piece of cake, that's because I didn't want to see you worried, but we did find it was quite nerve wracking and a bit scary!' That was the nice thing about Frank, he looked at my pal David and myself like two little brothers; after all, I was 18 and David was still only 17 at the time. The following year, 1965, Frank showed his funny side and his little bit crazy side, when we all went away to Aldershot for a few days to do regimental exercise, which included 4 parachute jumps over Hankley Common, Aldershot. We first embarked at Oxfordshire to take off in an aircraft and parachute over Hankley Common. One aircraft had already taken off and the paratroopers had done their jumps; however, the weather changed for the worst, so our group, which was about to take off in a Hastings aircraft was cancelled, so we drove to Aldershot in vehicles, where we were to do three balloon jumps. The next evening, we assembled at Hankley Common for a night jump from a balloon. We had our parachutes already on ready to go up, next in line, so our little group of five were getting ready to get into the cage when it was cancelled off. The wind force had got up, so night jumps in that sense were extra dangerous. It is more difficult to assess your direction and adjust your chute if need be. I was a bit disappointed to miss the experience. But the next day was a bit more eventful.

Steel helmets are useful

We left Aldershot to arrive at Hankley Common for two balloon jumps each. Now the chutes were all in a nearby truck so we put on our parachutes and steel helmets and were waiting around in little groups to take our turn. Putting on my steel helmet, I was about to learn a big lesson. The steel helmet had a chin strap like a pouch that snugly fits over and around the chin. There was a further strap that buckled up, also going around the back of the neck and back up to the chin strap to stabilize the helmet, giving a firm support. For some reason, I decided that hooking the chin piece onto my chin would be good enough. As we were waiting around in little groups, my pal David spotted it from where he was sitting on the ground leaning up against his parachute. Looking up at me he said, 'Your strap's not done up. Why don't you do it up properly?' Funny how you can remember things in such detail, so I looked down at him without even thinking very much about what he had just said. I said, 'No, it's ok. It will be alright.' Silly, really, especially as we were waiting around – I could easily have had time to correct and buckle it up properly. However, after a short wait it was our turn to enter the balloon cage and heed the command which is 'Up 800 feet – five men jumping', the normal command for the balloon to be released and guided by the cable up to 800 feet. Then it stops, there's a slight jerk, then silence. A balloon is such a cold blooded piece of kit. These days I would not like to go up and come down just for the ride, let alone jump out of one! Even if it meant having a good look around at the view, and pulled back down to earth ... No Thanks! But then let's go back again to May 1965. Up in the balloon, it's very eerie, spooky and the silence is deafening, except a slight rustle of breeze flapping against the barrage balloon. Five lads have suddenly all lost their voices, but then it's your turn to step forward. For the moment, this time, I believe I may have lost my focus, as I remember the dispatcher was going to have a right go at me, as he decided my approach to the doorway was incorrect.

He started to bellow at me and all I wanted to do was get to the doorway and exit as quick as possible to get it over with. He was going to have none of that... so I had to go back and do everything correctly and stand in the doorway, then jump on the order of command. Eventually, I jumped, but I lost my focus after being so bellowed at... Why couldn't he have said something useful, like tell me to buckle my helmet up properly? What a cheapskate he was... It all may have caused me to be a little late adjusting my parachute. As I was coming down a sudden gust of wind caught hold of the chute, sending me backwards, giving me no time to make any adjustments to the situation. Fortunately, I remembered my training and tucked myself up into my elbows, my head pushing down onto the reserve chute on my chest, legs slightly bent, ready to hit the ground and roll into a ball, in whatever direction required, which happened to be the very worst one... I crashed onto the ground very hard, going backwards, onto my head...helmet hitting the ground and taking the impact... The helmet saved me from possible serious injury. The force of the impact, though, caused the helmet to spin off along the ground for about 20 feet, all because it wasn't secured properly... I felt very embarrassed and sheepish about it all as I rolled up the chute, took it off... and went across to pick up the helmet. I then examined it to find a small dent shaped like a dimple. It so happened that a senior officer had been watching the whole event unfold, and taking note. It's possible he could even have heard from the ground the dispatcher in the balloon cage having a right go at me. He then came over; he had already recognised me as one of the boxers in the boxing team, soon to take part in the Regimental Championships a week or two later.

He looked at me and said, 'Right, young White, it's regiment boxing next week. You will not be going up again to do another jump. We cannot afford you to pick up an injury.'

However, crazy Frank Eagon, as funny as ever, he was watching it all and heard all that was going on, and the next thing, he was running down to the truck that holds the parachutes, to be collected as required, and he calls out, 'Right, one less jump means one spare parachute. What a waste!' says Frank, and looking over to me he says, 'Right Dave, your chute won't be wasted, it's going for a good cause.' Quick as a flash, he's got the chute on and going up for his third jump. I don't remember shedding any tears. There are some who jump from a balloon because they're under orders (I'm one of those) and some that volunteer to jump for the sheer fun of it (I wouldn't be one of those!). Let's say, being a little crazy may help and Frank was definitely one of those.

Ten para boxing and Sergeant Graves

Back at White City Headquarters, we often had regular paratroopers from 3 Para. Sometimes, officers or sergeants would work with 10 Para. One such was a sergeant from 3 Para, Sergeant Graves. A thick set, very tough looking man and not to be crossed. One time was when we were having a lesson on dismantling a sten gun. He looked, or should I say, glared at me over something I seemed not to be doing right. He quickly came over and I thought I was going to get it, as he looked angry, red faced and about to lose his temper. As quick as a flash, in the same moment, he seemed to change and deal with me a little different, as if to say, 'he's only a 19-year kid, I had better ease off'. Anyway, I soon was to see a bit of a soft centre in this tough paratrooper. He became a bit of a chauffeur, driving me to White City Headquarters, where the boxing was taking place. I was completely on my own, so he stayed with me, even in my corner as my corner man, for a few fights. I remember one comment he said to me just looking across to the other corner, before the ring of the bell to start the first round; looking at the opponent, he then said in my ear, 'I don't like the look of him...go out and give him a good hiding!' It made me smile afterwards and I've not forgotten those words as I think it sums up this tough British paratrooper that he was. The same attitude that they have in combat, and he just wanted to psyche me up for the fight. A couple of weeks later I went on to win the Regiment Championships and also was awarded the medal for being the best Regiment Boxer, which seemed very nice at the time.

In 1965, quite a busy year, around 12 fights, winning the Southern Counties title… worst time though was at SE London Championships, Eltham Baths. The win would have meant a chance to box at The Royal Albert Hall again. In the meantime, I had to beat Alf Pillay, an experienced boxer, 22 years old and I was coming up for 19. In 1963 and again in 1964, Alf boxed a friend, Brian Packer. Brian went on to win the British National Title in 1963 and 1964, which was an amazing achievement. In 1964, I saw the fight at Eltham Baths that Brian had against Alf Pillay. Climbing into the ring, Alf with his Caribbean looks and bushy hair, reminded me a little of Jimi Hendrix… Brian was favourite to win; however, Alf was a very plucky boxer with a chin like granite, he even knocked Brian down in the second round. He stood up to Brian well, considering that Brian was a terrific boxer with a hard punch in both hands. Not only did Brian win the National Title a second time in 1964, but he was an international boxer and would represent Britain in the 1964 Olympic Games. His only loss was to the eventual Gold Medal winner, Japanese boxer Takao Sakurai. He lost on a split decision, one of the judges voted Brian the winner. I would meet Alf Pillay myself in 1965 and at some stage before meeting him, Brian Packer confided in me that Alf Pillay gave him his hardest time, winning the British Title. The fight was eventful, except the result. Looking back it's all now a bit of a blur. I just remember the start of the fight going across the ring around my normal quick speed, and trying to knock Alf off his stride so that he would not settle, just throwing plenty of punches. However, I have included comments from the newspapers about the event, which may be of interest, and just about sums it all up.

Boxing

Swift loses title

DARTFORD A.B.C.'s reputation slipped a notch on Monday when light-middleweight Ray Swift lost his title in the S.E. divisional championships at Eltham Baths to younger, stronger Mark Rowe (Fitzroy Lodge).

The contest was stopped in the second round after Swift had been down twice in the first round from savage body blows and once in the second.

Dartford's other hope, wee Davey White, in a rugged bantam-weight contest, clubbed his way through three rounds, but a doubtful decision went to Alf Pillay (Lynn).

1965

oxing

AN ODD DECISION AT ELTHAM

DAVID WHITE was the victim of some peculiar judging at the South-East divisional championships at Eltham Baths on Monday. And that is putting it mildly.

White, Dartford's hard-punching bantamweight, swarmed all over Lynn's Alf Pillay and drilled a never-ending stream of right-hands into the face of the coloured southpaw.

I thought the decision would be a mere formality. White outpointed Pillay; but it was not to be. Pillay got the verdict and Eltham Baths erupted with anger and disbelief.

Pillay looked surprise — as well he might have. White? He just moped dejectedly from the ring a justifiably quizzical look on his countenance.

It was a terrible decision and one that could put a boy off boxing for good. I hope White will not be too discouraged by this setback.

Light-middle Ray Swift met his match and more in the efficient Mark Rowe (Fitzroy). Swift was down three times from wicked punching before the referee saved him from further punishment in the second round of their final. Rowe, who himself comes from Dartford, completely outgunned the tough Swift.

Only Dartford winner was cruiser, Brian Hall, who won the heavyweight title last year. Hall outpointed Les Barratt (Lynn) in a scrambling and messy final.

Flyweight Kabol Singh was stopped in the third round of his semi-final against J. Fitzgerald (Fitzroy).

Middleweight Ernie Longhurst was unable to box because of food poisoning.

C.D.

1965

BOXING

Small, cheerful - looking Kent Champion Dave White is known for his "little boy lost" approach to a bout. Many a tall lad has thought him an easy match until they have felt the power of his "dig."

Before a bout he sits in the corner, head hung down, looking very innocent, and giving curt replies to any questions. Then gloves well up he goes in and explodes into a bundle of fury. His name is now so well-known that when he goes to an open match Club secretaries are wary of matching their boys against him.

1965

SEACADET BOXING TEAM JUST BEFORE THE INTERSEAVICES & JUNIOR ABA QUARTER FINALS 1962.

1962...Brian Packer and my self.

RETURN BOUT FOR WHITE

David White, the Dartford boxer, has secured with comparative ease a return fight with Alf Pillay (Lynn) at Bermondsey on April 26.

Pillay scored a hotly-disputed points win over him in the S.E. divisional championships in March.

Bantamweight White got in some useful practice when appearing in a Margate A.B.C. show on Friday.

He outpointed a taller and heavier R. Pym (Ruislip).

Crisp and classic was flyweight Kabol Singh's bout with Dave Roberts (Ruislip). Singh lost narrowly on points.

Not so picturesque was Pat Manning's scrappy affair with Roger Ralph (St. Mary's), but he won on points.

Junior results.—D. McKeon lost to A. Walton, of Earlsfield (bout stopped in first round), P. Marro outpointed by J. Foster (Crawley), B. Cooper beat M. O'Leary (Chiswick), r.s.f. second, T. O'Dwyer beat A. Forsythe (Crawley), retired second.

1965

After six weeks, we would meet again to settle the score, at Bermondsey, where we both had a point to prove. Alf wanted to show that beating me was no fluke. Myself, I don't believe I had any animosity until the bell went, and l quickly came over to Alf Pillay's corner like an angry little wasp, both of us throwing non-stop punches. I just felt at all costs, do or die, I just had to win, and I put all I had into the fight. It was absolutely electric from the start.

One funny moment in my mind that I remember clearly was, as the bell rung at the end of the first round and I turned to walk back to my corner, the stool came out, I plonked myself down…then I began to think…oh no, have I really got to get up and do that all over again, then the bell goes, and so do you, prepared to do it all over again, whatever it takes to win the fight.

It's like a re-run of a film, that particular fight anyway. Into the second round, after a short while, Alf stuck out his granite like chin just enough for me to put all my weight into a right hook and straight down he goes. For all the world, I didn't expect him to stir but on the count of four, he slowly started to rise, but then I was thinking my next funny thought, OH... 'no, no, stay down, you're not supposed to get up yet!'. But then he was up at the count of eight… and very soon after, the fight was stopped. Once again the newspaper clippings explain the fight in more accurate detail than I can. I have included them as they may be of interest.

Pillay Sees The Point

"Evening News" Reporter

DARTFORD'S dashing bantam prospect, Dave White, smashed his way to a second round win over Lynn southpaw, Alf Pillay, in a "needle" return contest on the Oxford and Bermondsey club show at the club hall, Pages-walk, Bermondsey.

Stocky White, current Southern Counties' champion, lost a hotly disputed decision to Pillay in the final of the S.E. London divisional championships at Eltham in March.

This time, however, he tore into the Lynn boy from the opening bell with vicious two fisted attacks to the head and body.

Long Reach

Smart Pillay used his superior height and reach to box his way out of trouble after overcoming White's whirlwind start, but winced with pain every time that the dour Dartford boy sank home his short hooks to the body.

Tearaway White continued his merciless and relentless aggression in the second, and gave game Pillay no respite before sending him crashing to the canvas with a right to the jaw.

Pillay found his feet at eight and fought back spiritedly but could not ward off the determined attacks of all-action White and was wisely rescued by the referee.

RESULTS: R Callaghan (Dog Kennel Hill) outptd J Doyle (Dartford); **P Manning** (Dartford) outptd R. Carroll (Downham Community); **J. Douglas** (Camberwell) stopped T. Constant (Catford) second; **B Ellis** (Dartford) outptd H Simms (Camberwell); **T McSweeney** (Catford) stopped B Groombridge (Printers) first; **D Middleton** (Catford) outptd T McNulty (St. Peters);

T Kavanagh (Stock Exchange) outptd E Baker (Catford); **R Cockett** (Lynn) outptd J Spencer (Catford); **J Jackson** (Fisher) outptd A Mills (Dog Kennel Hill); **J Gare** (Oxford and Bermondsey) outptd M Glynn (Downham Goldsmiths); **R Sulley** (Lynn) outptd J Boakes (Dartford); **D White** (Dartford) stopped **A Pillay** (Lynn) second.

1965

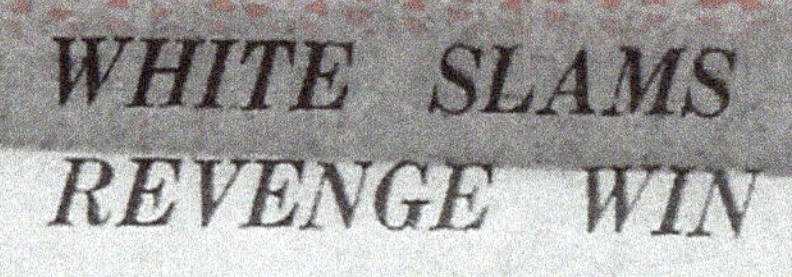

WHITE SLAMS REVENGE WIN

DARTFORD'S Dave White, a sturdy bantam prospect, gained revenge in convincing fashion for a hotly-disputed points loss to Lynn southpaw, Alf Pillay, in last month's S.E. London Divisional Championships, whe he stopped his rival in two rounds on the Oxford & Bermondsey club show, at the Club Hall, Pages Walk, Bermondsey.

Relentless White opened in tigerish fashion, slamming home hard two-fisted hooks to the head and body. The Lynn boy, overwhelmed by this whirlwind start, gamely tried to hit back but was frequently hurt by the Dartford boy's powerful body blows.

A power-laden right to the jaw sent Pillay crashing to the canvas in the second. He got to his feet at "eight", but was rescued by the referee soon afterwards with White pressing rome his advantage unmercifully.

RESULTS: **R. Callaghan** (Dog Kennel Hill outptd. J. Doyle (Dartford); **P. Manning** (Dartford) outptd. R. Carroll (Downham (Community); **J. Douglas** (Camberwell) stppd. T. Constant (Catford) second; **B. Ellis** (Dartford) outptd. H. Simms (Cambtrwell); **T. McSweeney** (Catford) stppd. B. Groombridge (Printers) first; **D. Middleton** (Catford) outptd. T. McNulty (St. Peters).

T. Kavanagh (Stock Exchange) outptd. E. Baker (Catford); **R. Cockett** (Lynn) outptd. J. Spencer (Catford); **J. Jackson** (Fisher) outptd. A. Mills (Dog Kennel Hill); **J. Gare** (Oxford and Bermondsey) outptd. M. Glynn (Downham Goldsmith); **R. Sulley** (Lynn) outptd. J. Boakes (Dartford); **D. White** (Dartford stppd. A. **Pillay** (Lynn) second.

1965

A cameo film role and meeting Henry Cooper

The summer of 1965 was a great time. It felt good being 19, still a teenager, a fun time. Around this time, in July, I got a phone call from Brian Packer, who kindly asked me if I wanted to appear on a programme with him for Southern Counties TV. He was a young up and coming boxer, as already mentioned of national fame in the boxing world and had just turned professional. The conversation went like this: 'Dave, do you want to be on a television programme? Southern Counties are doing a TV article on young and up and coming sports people and they're doing one on myself.' I said yes I was interested. Brian then said to get myself up to the Thomas a Becket gym in the Old Kent Road and we'd do a bit of boxing together in the ring. 'Be there tomorrow about 2pm. I'll be there with a TV crew.' So, I said yes OK that I'd be there. The next day I turned up with my trainer Norman Stanton. We spent a couple of hours together with the film crew and we all ended up going out and having a cup of tea... Downside… I never got to see the film, so I've often been curious about this short film story of Brian and my cameo role and what happened to it. It's either gathering dust or, more likely, been destroyed or thrown out.

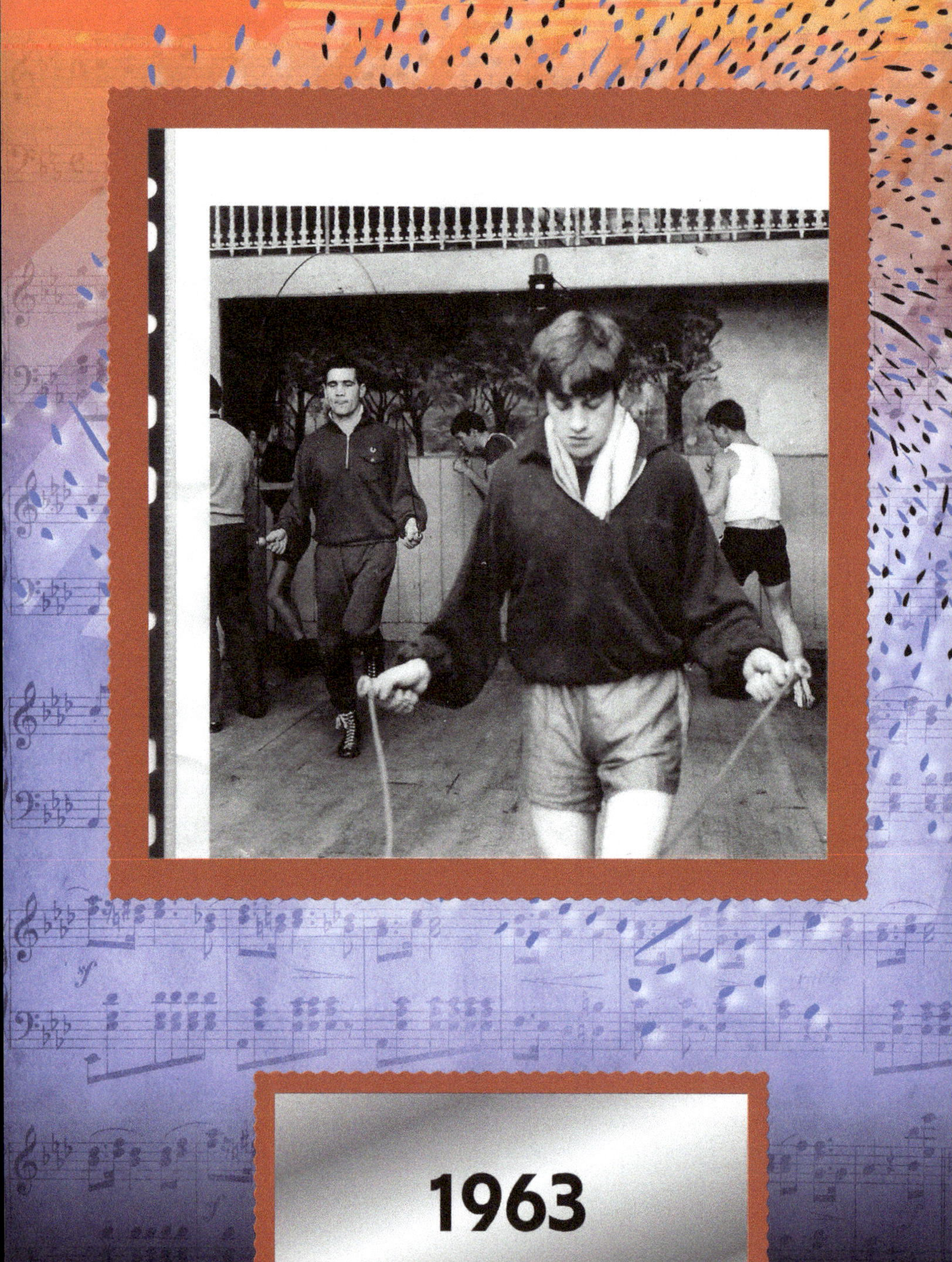

1963

While talking about the famous gym Thomas a Becket, and during the summer of 1965, another interesting incident, quite by accident... I went to the gym one afternoon with my trainer Norman. It was all very quiet and it seemed that no-one was around. As we climbed the stairs to access the gym, I turned into one of the doorways and the changing room, and there was Henry Cooper, just being rubbed down and then getting changed. He was with his manager and trainer, Jim Wicks. A short, bald headed stout man, nicknamed 'The Bishop'.

Norman exchanged 'hellos'. I felt very shy and nervous and did what I normally do and found a quiet corner and got changed. I then slid out into the gym, hoping not to be noticed. Invisible would be probably the best way to describe how I felt. Henry would have none of it... Within 10 minutes I was in my own little world on the punch bag, shadow boxing, and I dismissed Henry out of my mind. Suddenly, I sensed this large presence that would not move. I worked out after a while, that it was Henry, staring at me and the more I realised it, the more I just wanted him to clear off. I suddenly felt out of my comfort zone, and he would not move until he caught my eye, which meant then I had to look at him... He gave a lovely smile, a wink of his eye, a nod of the head and then the big man turned around, ambled towards the stairs and down he went, out on to the street. What a lovely man. Such courtesy. I thought a lot about that incident over the years. Henry was a world class boxer and little me, he would not have heard of, and yet in that moment he showed such courtesy and kindness. No one would have noticed if he had slid off out of the building without any kind of acknowledgement.

1965 seemed to tick along and I was still involved with 10 Para Regiment. I boxed a few times again. I enjoyed the year very much. On a personal level, though, my life was about to change anyway, and quickly.

Early in '66, I had a few fights just before the start of the National Championships in March. I injured my right hand and I know I was very silly. I tried to ignore it and hoped that it would go away. It would all start at the Southern Counties Championships. I thought I'd box in a higher weight division. It was the Semi Finals, a close fought fight and I lost on a points decision. However, I sustained and injured my right hand... but then late in February, I happened to have a fight at Battersea Town Hall and it was a good win against the London Champion and England International boxer. After the fight I knew that I had done my injured hand no favours and now it was even more damaged, but I never considered it was serious enough to lose any sleep over it, let alone mention it to anyone. I just thought it was badly bruised and if I didn't use it for a week or two, I'd be able to carry on regardless. But the fight I had at Battersea Town Hall was quite a scrap and after the fight, I knew my hand was more than just bruised, but I thought, still again, I've got National Championships coming up in two weeks and also a week before the start of the championships, I was committed to do this job training scheme. It was to do with my present employment at the time. You end up feeling committed and more bothered about letting people down, and those close to you, such as the club and various people, other boxers involved and of course my trainer Norman who was a good friend. All that seemed more important than what you wanted to do. On the day of the fight, I went through the normal routine of preparing myself, trying to just ignore the injury in the hope that it would stand up. The hands were bandaged, as you do. When the fight began, for a start, I was not my normal self.... like I had the brakes on. I was slightly hesitant. My brain for once was trying to rule my body. When I started to throw punches I suddenly landed one on my opponent's forehead, which immediately felt like an explosion in my right fist. Almost immediately, I just dropped down on one knee in shock.

I knew I was in trouble and I just wanted a second or two to gather my thoughts and of course, carry on, perhaps with one hand. I would never consider quitting, but the decision was made for me. The referee decided that there was a problem, took me back to my corner and would not let me continue. For that moment, I felt absolutely gutted. Of course, I felt the referee overreacted. It was not possible for him to know my real problem, unless he was a mind reader, so ... If need be, I would have carried on as best I could with one good hand, but as can happen with boxers, decisions are often made for you. As I left the ring, it was as if it was yesterday, it's so clear in my head. I felt as if I was in total shock. Though I was not blubbing out loud, I just could not stop the floods of tears running down my face… like a quiet Niagara Falls. I noticed my vest was getting soaking wet and even onto my boxing gloves. (Not a good look for a boxer.) My reaction stunned me really, as I wasn't aware of it happening. I felt rather embarrassed, all that water and not able stop floods of tears running down my face. It felt like it was not me in that ring, and what had just happened. I felt so ashamed, that I had let so many people down… Of course, you get over these things. There are other more important things in life than boxing that were on the horizon. But I just have to say, strangely enough, I have, in 50 years, never ever been able to speak about that incident. I've always avoided it, so putting it in writing helps lay it to rest. Funny though, at the time, everyone around me never harped on about it, as if they accepted it was just one of those things and you move on. When the gloves were taken off, my right hand had swollen up like a football. It turned out I had a broken knuckle bone and it was pushed back into my hand… By 1967, my boxing was behind me. I never thought that much of myself anyway, I was insecure and lacked confidence in my ability. However, my sister Joan a few years ago reminded me of that… She told me that when I was young I was very insecure.

I thought about it for some time afterwards and realised that she was right… She also told me an interesting little story of when her husband, who went to the same golf club as Norman, my ex trainer – they would have a drink together and on this occasion at the Lullingstone Golf Club, they then got onto the subject of boxing, and talked about various boxers, and all this was probably over 25 years or more after I had stopped boxing. Norman would tell my brother-in-law, in the course of the conversation, that he thought myself, David White, was the best little boxer that he ever knew. My brother-in-law told my sister when he got home and my sister Joan told me sometime later about the conversation. For a moment, when she told me, that really stunned me; it held more value than any newspaper clippings I still have. I considered that Norman, my trainer, was himself a good boxer and a very good trainer. But still, I couldn't think I was that good or that that kind of praise was deserved.

With club secretary
Len Baker
1964

DAVID WHITE FEATHER WEIGHT BOXER
LONDON 1966

Boxing from the age of 12 had always been the core of my life, but from 17, I had three personal incidents that I believe would have an effect on me and tarnish my feelings towards my chosen sport. It was not common for a doctor to enter a boxing ring. I cannot think back and remember any occasion, except three that I was personally involved in at 17, 18 and 19. From 12-16, boxing was a lot of fun and about comradeship and friendship. You'd always box boys around your own weight and age. It was strictly monitored. I would say there was a lot of good done to help young boys. It would channel their natural aggression. It taught them to respect each other and those around them. From 17, things would change. Boys were turning into young men and it's alarming the power from these athletes that they could and would exert on one another. I can say that on a personal level… Late 1963, one evening at Bethnal Green, I was to meet a 21-year old boy who was the Essex Champion and in the second round I landed a hard punch and flush on the jaw, he would lie on the ring floor for 20 minutes, with a doctor hovering over him.

After 10 minutes, I remember my trainer and ex professional boxer George Pyne, getting me out of the ring and away from the scene, not wanting to talk to me about it. The club would be concerned about the young man, that he would recover, but I know he was whisked away to hospital by ambulance, and stayed there overnight.

Today it is mandatory that a doctor is always present at boxing shows and any evidence of concussion, even if it's not a knock-out blow, boys would go to hospital for a brain scan. If that boy had not recovered, I am sure that I would not have boxed again. At 17, and young, you accept he must be ok and we all move on with our lives. You don't ask too many questions. At 18, in Maidstone, the following year, during the Kent finals, a similar incident would happen again. A hard punch was delivered and the boy went out cold. Within a few minutes, a doctor was hovering over him. Eventually, he recovered. By then, I'm long gone out of the ring. You're kind of switched off, but it still registered within you. At 19, a year later, at Basildon, Essex. Again, a similar incident, I went across the ring and landed a heavy punch. The boy was flat out. No count was needed, except the doctor, who climbed into the ring to assist. He eventually recovered, thank goodness. What happened to these three lads, I don't know? I trust and hope they never boxed again. It all had some effect on me; I don't mean a blinding light on the road to Damascus. It would take a bit longer than that – as a teenager, you are enjoying your life – but even then I had a problem if I saw someone hurt, it would stay with you, more so if you are responsible. You cannot totally bury such feelings. You are what you are.

Baroness Edith Summerskill vs Henry Cooper!

Boxing has always been controversial as a sport. A few lonely voices in the wilderness have expressed their displeasure. One in particular was Baroness Edith Summerskill, an MP, who not only voiced her disdain for the sport, but tried her best to have it banned during the 1960s, especially in the schools, at grassroots level, which was then a part of every school's curriculum. This would lead to what become a very funny exchange that took place with British Heavyweight Champion Henry Cooper. In 1970, a meeting of the two was set up by the BBC. They would meet up on TV; Henry to discuss the virtues of boxing and how it did not do him any harm etc. and Edith, who would be around 70 years old, and a long way off from being an oil painting, in her Les Dawson bonnet. She would voice her disdain for the injuries and damage caused by an accumulation of punches and then suddenly at one stage of the conversation, Edith Summerskill said to Henry, 'Have you looked in the mirror recently at your nose? Well? Have you?' For a second or two Henry thought about her remark and replied, 'Well, with respect, have you looked in the mirror? I got my nose through boxing…what's your excuse?!' Every so often, just like a comedy sketch, that film clip of the interview would be wheeled out, aired, and replayed to the nation, to cheer everybody up. However, it has to be said, though Edith Summerskill was not taken too seriously by many people, there is no doubt she was influential in banning boxing being taught in schools around the year 1962.

DAVID, AGE 12
1958

The end of boxing

By 1967 my time in boxing had come to an end, and I met my future wife Evelyn, who was one of Jehovah's Witnesses. I knew she would be a good wife, but she took a chance with me. I was known as a boxer and certainly not as one of Jehovah's Witnesses at that stage. I must have shown genuine interest and started going to Bible meetings. We married late in 1967. Slowly, I got involved in the faith, and was baptized as one of Jehovah's Witnesses in 1968. I was 22 years of age. During the 1970s, we would have four children: Maria in 1970, Tony in 1974, Ricky in 1976 and Wayne in 1979. Perhaps this is a good time for me to say how I became one of Jehovah's Witnesses. It became the second core of my life. Being a boxer was the centre of my life but once I became one of Jehovah's Witnesses, that took over and became my main focus. Although I have to say being a J.W. is often not easy, especially knocking on doors and talking to strangers about our faith. It's something you feel you can only do if you believe you have found the truth and the meaning and a purpose to life, one that holds out a wonderful future for mankind.

The journey, to reach that point, I'm sure would have been from an early age, perhaps when I was 8 years old... I know I had a spiritual side, and realised that it's something that's built into everybody, unlike animals or plants. We all have this need to know why we are on the earth, we love life and living, and yet why do we have so much trouble and problems throughout our life? As we look at others around us and of course, worldly governments that cannot agree, people's lives are affected at every level, whether it's medical care, education, violence and immorality. It's always been the same, true, but since the 1950s, it's steadily increased into epidemic proportions, affecting all generations and individuals in a negative way.

Becoming one of Jehovah's Witnesses

I want to avoid this section of the mini book being a little 'preachy' etc. Everyone needs to make their own decisions about their lives. Where they want to go with it. But I'm sure there's nothing wrong with a little helping hand along the way. I personally believe that I have found that, and the same invitation is offered to all.

Around 1954, as an eight-year old, my parents studied the Bible with Jehovah's Witnesses. They had a lot of questions, and they felt that a Bible Study would help. I would have been around, if only in the background, so I picked up on many things said. I liked the sound of living in a Paradise Earth, no wars or illnesses, people able to live and not die, not get old. To many of course, it would sound 'pie in the sky', but you quickly learn, that really was God's original purpose, and not a fairy story. The book of Genesis quickly explains that.

Twickenham
Audience listenning to the
Convention,

Twickenham convention 1955 and 1956

As previously mentioned Mum and Dad around the mid-50s, were having a Bible study. They were also invited along to the assembly convention at Twickenham in the mid-1950s… I am grateful they took me along, though it would not be until the end of the 1960s before I went along to a Twickenham convention for myself… As a young boy of just nine or ten years old and still at primary school, it would all leave a lasting impression, so many 1000s of peaceful and kind people getting on with one another… The three photographs bring the memory flooding back, the wee Scottish boy we would play with and go around together for a short time. Unfortunately, his name escapes me, not so Christopher. I studied the photo recently, the first time in some 60 years, and his name came flooding back.

1955 .Twickenham
convention
Lunch.
David,Mum,Fay,Joan.

1955. 9 Years old.
Making friends with little
scottish boy..
Twickenham convention.

10 years old, making friends with boy named Christopher at Twickenham convention.
1956

Little Austin 7 van

We are sitting down having lunch at the back of the motor. The little 1937 Austin 7 van was a very funny motor, with a wooden body, wire spoke wheels and squeaky brakes. The driver's door was not too clever either – if not properly shut and you're going around a left hand bend, it may fly open, and Dad's arm would have to dive after it at 40 miles per hour. He would learn that positioning his elbow along the door in the right position would help hold everything in place…until he would forget…

School's helping hand

I have good memories of saying The Lord's Prayer every morning in school assembly, before the start of lessons. We would all gather in a large hall, bow our heads and say the prayer that we knew off by heart, from repetition. It was a spiritual start to the day that would help you to reflect, if not that day, perhaps later in life. It was the words especially that would later enable you to grasp some meaning to life. Even as an eight-year old I connected them to the Bible Study my parents were having. The Bible-based books and magazines that were around the house helped to explain the significance of the Lord's Prayer. For instance, 'hallowed be thy name' signifies that the priority is to sanctify God's name. The first thing that a person learns in a study, is that God has a personal name, Jehovah, and that it should be in the Bible over 7,000 times. You have to know that name in order to 'hallow' or sanctify it. That name actually means 'He causes to become' which means anything that God purposes will come about.

At dinnertime, we would offer up a prayer before sitting down to eat. This was known as grace. It was always the same words 'For what we are about to receive, may the Lord make us truly grateful'. I know it is repetition, but it taught us children respect and manners, in offering thanks to a creator, the giver and provider of food. More appreciation for all these things may come with time.

The other important fact, and it's what all mankind needs, is God's Kingdom. In The Lord's Prayer, we pray for that Kingdom to come. At a very early age, I learned that 'kingdom' is another name for 'government' and by means of this perfect government or kingdom, with Jesus as its King, mankind will all eventually be brought back to God's original purpose of living in a perfect environment. This reign will last for 1,000 years.

Even the millions of dead, in memorial tombs, will be resurrected to life and have the opportunity of living forever on a restored earth.

Until I was around eight years of age, I was attending Sunday School at the local church, but it would be Jehovah's Witnesses who helped to explain the meaning of the Lord's Prayer. To this day, the whole prayer is a wonderful reflection of Jehovah God and his son Jesus, as it outlines God's purpose for the earth and how we can have a share in that purpose.

Though not brought up as one of Jehovah's Witness, and having kept it at arms-length until my early 20s, even so, I just knew they spoke the truth and applied it as best they could in their own lives.

On a personal level, I've noticed that every Jehovah's Witness is a unique individual, as we should all be, and my friends have all come from all sorts of backgrounds, yet we are completely united in our faith, which motivates us to serve our Creator unitedly, without divisions. Families are also very loving and caring with one another. All this from people who, though not perfect, are willing to try to improve as required.

I hope I continue to apply these sentiments to myself, as I endeavour to continue to be a part of a worldwide group of Christian people, at total peace with one another.

Swanley Junction finally grows up…a personal view

By 1940 war clouds over England were quickly forming… My grandad Tom White wanted to move his family of six children away from the dangers of London… Nan and Grandad were typical tough cockneys from the heart of the East End…Shoreditch and Hoxton area. They knew living by the docks would make them a vital target area for enemy aircraft.

Grandad would organise a house to rent for the family in Swanley, being around 15 miles as the crow flies…or Heinkel bomber from the east end of London… They got to know the Swanley area from the casual farm work they would do during the 1930s. As many other Londoners did too...it would mean some extra cash. Farmers would have erected tin huts to live in for the summer duration, until the end of August, then they would move on for Hop-picking, to a chosen Hopfield farm further down in Kent. Grandad was an upholsterer by trade, and during the farming season in Kent would stay in the London East End area at his workshop during the week, then journey down to Kent, normally on a push bike for the weekend, to catch up with his family.

Going back home to the East End may have been a little wobbly though, taking place on the Sunday, after supping and downing a few pints of brown ale to ease the long journey back home.

Once war got under way in 1940 he would then spend the next six years in the army as a dispatch rider and being among the first troops to liberate the Channel Islands... Though Grandad has been gone now for some 28 years....and yet for some time before he passed away, and many years before the TV Documentaries and the many books written about the five years of German occupation, he seldom would speak of his experiences of the time he helped to liberate the Channel Islands during 1945; however...he was known to say how desperate the whole situation was, food fast running out for the Islanders, and German soldiers alike, food and conditions were only progressing very slowly towards steady improvement... Grandad would say how hungry and emaciated everyone was.

The British soldiers would share their own rations with Islanders and Germans alike.

These days, yet not surprising, the Islanders have chosen to retain the German defences, underground military hospital, and many interesting artefacts, as a constant reminder of the occupation, all still within living memory. Also, it is quite a tourist attraction for British and Germans alike.

I have visited the Channel Islands myself, three times in the last 10 years, and seen most of the concrete defences where large guns were in place. You can just walk around freely. There are a few other sites that are conducted by a short guided tour and explanation with military artefacts to look at. There was one funny incident that did happen to me around five years ago, so would be 2011.

There happened to be a very large gun defence battery connected by concrete tunnels you would have been able to walk along; I suppose, maybe there could have been 100 German soldiers involved and billeted on this gun battery… As I climbed the concrete steps up to where the gun emplacement would have been was a very large concrete base, where many people could stand around if need be. In this instance there was a large group of German-speaking people, average age was probably 65-70.

They were speaking in a very excited way, gesturing, and some laughing at what was being said, and of course I could not understand a word of it; however, like a switch going down as soon as they saw me, and, likely, they instantly assumed I was English…Everything went quiet, they looked slightly sheepish, then I realised they were probably on a tour holiday too where their fathers had been stationed during the Second World War.

A funny thought then went through my head. It made me think of a tour agency deep in the heart of Germany and a holiday advert… (This is said in a very tongue-in-cheek, Monty Python way) Advert reads… THE FATHERLAND WOULD LIKE TO ARRANGE A WONDERFULL HOLIDAY ON THE SUNNY WARM CHANNEL ISLANDS. FOR THE CHILDREN OF THE GERMAN SOLDIERS STATIONED THERE. It was a lovely five years stay and we did not want to come home.

However, the British Army were ever so polite, they said please, please, can we have our islands back… We, of course, made sure we had the last word… "You may have your Channel Islands back, Englanders, but only if you feed us first…

And of course the rest is history… which is still there if you want to go and have a look for yourselves…

Back to Swanley Junction

My dad, like Grandad, was also named Tom... and a very cheeky cockney boy, at 15 could not wait to get into uniform and take on Hitler. However, all he could do at the time was join the local home guard, and help take care of Swanley Junction, the High Street, and especially the railway station, where Winston Churchill was known to embark or disembark and then be chauffer driven in his limousine to Chartwell near to Westerham.

Once Dad received his home guard uniform he felt unsatisfied with the baggy fit and length of the trousers, so swiftly he went to work with a pair of scissors and a lot of imagination, then ending up with a desecrated uniform with one trouser leg longer than the other. Never mind, he thought, if the enemy attack at night they may never notice.

However, as we all know, imagination can be a wonderful thing, if perhaps at times a little dangerous…

Not satisfied with marching, and patrolling around Swanley Junction … at around 16 years of age he learned his young uncle Ted, my nan's brother, was a part of the newly formed parachute regiment; in fact Ted a few years later on would be taken prisoner of war at the battle of Arnhem, in Holland.

In no time Dad located the regiment, and by putting up his age by two years would join up. However, Ted would have none of it – as soon as he clapped eyes on his young nephew Tom he gave him a right telling off, and informed his sister Violet, Dad's mum, who promptly arrived to frog march him back home… as she did, in her parting cockney accent calling out "you can't ave im e's still only a boy"…

Hitler would have to wait a little longer to be dealt with… in the meantime the people of Swanley Junction would sleep safely in their beds at night as Dad continued to patrol and march along Swanley Junction… with his specially adapted broomstick handle over his shoulder.

Mum (Joan) 18 years old
1944

Dad (Tom White) 19 year old .
6th. Airborne...
1944.

1944. Preparing for combat.
Dad is 5th para on left.

And once again...back to Swanley Junction

Once those war clouds over the country had gone, as already previously mentioned, Swanley would grow at an alarming pace, with all the many housing estates springing up, an ideal location still, for people working in London... By rail you could be in the centre of London within the hour; on the other hand, at the weekends, if you felt like a walk in the opposite direction, within the hour you could be in the beautiful Kent countryside, and some lovely villages. What an amazing contrast. Though I may have inherited a little London in my blood, I know where I really love to be and the countryside of Kent takes some beating.

Later, of course, motorways such as the M20, M2 and M25 etc, all close to London, would give drivers more scope...though, I feel some of the countryside has been sacrificed. However, it would seem many of the local villages and towns have benefited by keeping lots of heavy traffic at bay.

If we all wants our cars, and the flow of lorries to service shopping centres, with the needed goods, it would seem that some of the countryside in our present environment will be sacrificed, it may be 'the price to pay', perhaps the victims of our own so called success, unless we return back to the horse and cart...

At least to some extent, villages and small towns such as Swanley have benefited from these road systems allowing them to be relatively unspoilt, as main traffic is diverted around and not through their own backyard.

However, as we know, it can be a devil to park anywhere at times and with still so many vehicle restrictions imposed, does not help… The jury remains out on that problem…

By the 1960s, Swanley Junction had moved on to become a small town. It would not remain a one horse cowboy looking town any more…

Though I have often remembered how well contained it was for much of all your needs such as Butcher's, Greengrocer's, Clothes shops, newsagent's, fishmonger's, ironmonger's, builders' merchants, bicycle shops, cafes etc etc, probably I have left off a few other small businesses. The crowning glory of the 1960s was probably the Co-Op Stores – they seemed to sell just about everything especially household goods and electrical goods such as TVs, radios, record players and so on…

As Swanley grows into the 1970s, the Corona Cinema would be demolished. It was opened in 1938, a lovely building, inside and out, built in the art deco style.

The area would be replaced and become Swanley precinct… The Swanley Junction tag had gone forever – of course it would happen anyway into the 1960's – it was by far outgrowing the junction part of its name.

If you were born in Swanley in the 1940s and 50s, parents and children would often use the phrase 'up the junction' such as, see you later just going up the junction, or Mum would say 'would you go up the junction for some shopping?' so up the junction used in all its different forms would be a familiar sound… However, I believe the sudden demise of 'up the junction' saying, happened after one evening during the middle of a 1965 TV documentary drama, rather political and risqué in its content and names 'up the junction'.

As if overnight that saying would be left off in conversation with Swanley people, it would become 'just off up to Swanley' or maybe 'see you later, just going to the shops'.

It was that familiar saying 'up the junction' among Swanley people that would finally receive its final death knell from the 1965 TV drama. But for old times' sake, I want to 'Go up the junction' one more time and how appropriate, as I have considered a railway theme to end the journey, with some photographs…after all that was what Swanley Junction was all about…100 years ago…

The old Railway station around 1900.

The new Swanley Railway station
1939.

New Swanley Railway station with steam train 1939.

New Swanley Railway station with eletctric train 1939.

The old Swanley station 1900.

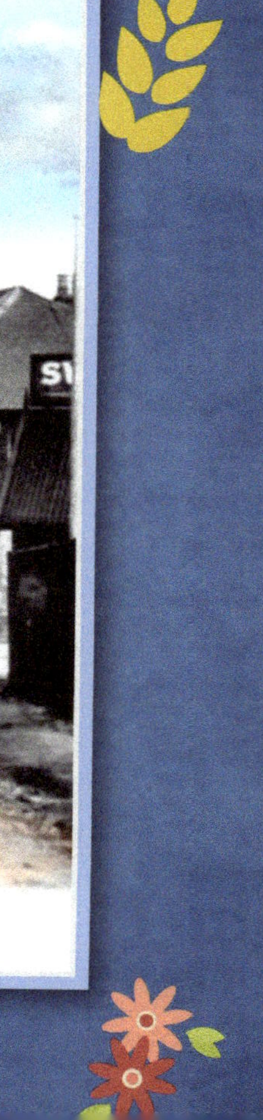

STATION ROAD, SWANLEY.

1910

ST Road Swanley
1910...

High Street, Swanley

Swanley High ST.
1910

Lower Swanley Junction High St
1910

Kingwood Church
botton end of high st ,
Swanley
1906

1935
Swanley high st

1936 Railwaybridge
at Goldsel Rd, 2years before iron
foot bridge.

Lorry crash on to Swanley bridge
1935

Report on the Accident at Swanley Junction on 27th June 1937

"The 8.17 a.m. up passenger train (steam), Margate to Victoria, via Canterbury West, Ashford, and Maidstone East, travelling at considerable speed, passed Swanley Junction home signal (platform starter) in the danger position, and came into violent collision with a loaded goods wagon and an empty 2-coach bogie set, which were standing in the short up (run-off) siding at the London end of the station. The train was running late and out of course; it was due to pass Swanley Junction at 10.52 p.m., but it was intended to stop it specially to pick up a number of passengers who had missed their normal connection (the preceding up branch electric train).

There were some 100 passengers in the train, and I regret to report that four sustained fatal injuries. Eleven other passengers were injured and taken to hospital, eight of them being detained; 36 others also complained of minor injuries or shock, of whom eight sustained cuts or bruises when subsequently rendering assistance. [The driver] and [the fireman] had remarkable escapes; but they evidently suffered severely from shock, and the latter, who was also slightly injured, could not remain at duty."

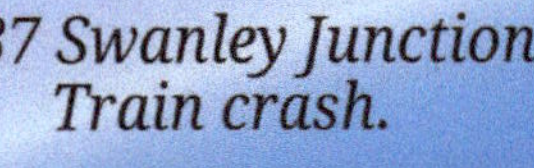
1937 Swanley Junction Train crash.

1937 Swanley Junction Train crash.

Swanley traffic lights 1935

Building the 2 iron bridges
1938
Swanley high st

1935
bottom end
Swanley High St…

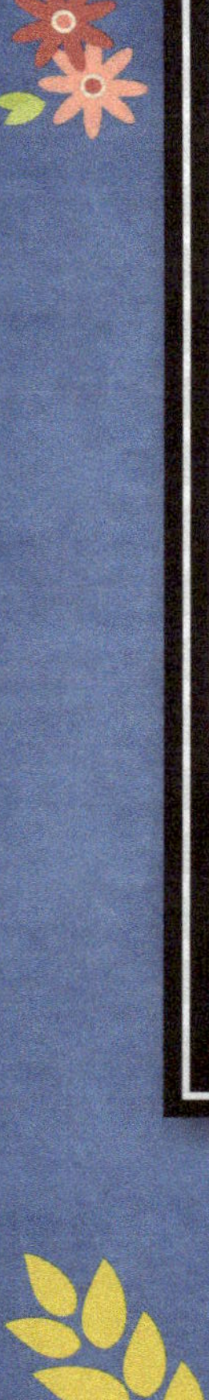

1940,s
Iron clad bridge,
looking up towards Corona
Cinema

Corona Cinema built
1938
Demolished 1970.

Corona Cinema, Swanley
Image courtesy of Cinema Theatre Association

In side the Corona

1951..
Swanley High St With ...
Corona Cinema, in background.

1956, opp. kingwood church
Waiking towards the
high st. Swanley,

Nan and Grandad… the legacy

1940, war had already been declared; however, there was a period of time known as the phoney war when nothing very much seemed to be happening, until the British troops were pushed back at Dunkirk. People then would start to sit up and notice how vulnerable England was. Grandad, before that stage, felt that way, though not known as a very political man, had somehow managed to convince Nan of the serious danger she would be in to stay in London with the children. He was about to go into the army for the next six years and wanted to know his family would be safe and secure…Of course many other cities in the country received bomb damage especially if they had military connections or were ports, harbours, with merchant and naval ships… with London, once the bombing began in 1940 it went on night after night for five years, known as the London Blitz, with little respite, and then of course in the last six months of the war it would be the V rockets' turn. No one could know just how bad and long it all would be including Grandad – even so, he was bang on the money; such wisdom for a young man of 35 years.

You cannot over dramatize the horror of it all, the part of London the family would escape from, close to the docks would be bombed and completely flattened… However, Grandad would find a place for them to all be together. Few families from London were able to do that; often families became split, some living in perhaps different parts of the country, throughout the war and not all getting back together again for perhaps four or five years.

You cannot rule out Grandad's action of moving the family away from London's East End may not only have saved their lives, but also secured a home for them to all be together… And for Grandad when he came home from the army to settle down in …

The legacy…….

Good news for the happy hoppers

Deep in the heart of the Kent countryside the farmer has given Nan her hopping hut for another year… In the photo, Grandad is seen on one of his usual weekend visits… Around the glowing embers of an outdoor kitchen he has just finished reading the Financial Times, and, to cheer Nan up, he tells her some good news… 'Well Vi, I've just done my annual inspection of the amenities on the common… Still no running water in the huts, no electricity or lights, no flushing toilets…no main drainage, and the toilets are the same tin huts as last time. But there is good news… The hop shares have risen… it looks like you've got your hut for a few more years…

Nan is overcome with joy…

Nan and Grandad the
Happy Hoppers
Goudhurst, kent
1952.

Mum,Nan,Hoppicking
Early 1950,s.

Mum and sister Joan
hoppicking
1950

Fay & David
Broadstairs
1951

David & Joan
1960

Fay and Mum

Evelyn ,(16)Lowerstoft
1960

1963
Maurice with 2 sons and
Susan
Twickenham Convention.

1970
Maurice and Vicky
at back
Twickenham Convention.

Mum, Dad,
with
Joan and husband
David
1971

Fay and Marion
Mid 1980,s

Marion.s wedding 1987
Joan. Marion .Mum.
Fay .Pearl.

Evelyn & David Wedding
1967

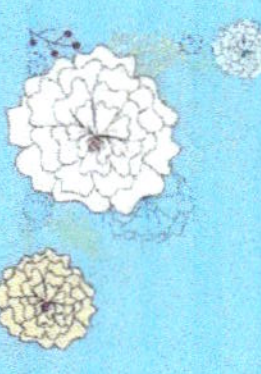

DAVID & EVELYN
1967.

EVELYN & HER MUM & DAD
1967

The Tribe 1996
Maria,David, Evelyn,
Wayne,
Ricky,Tony,

SWANLEY CONGREGATION 1966
EVELYN IN CENTRE OF PHOTO IN WHITE DRESS.

SWANLEY CONGREGATION
2014

SWANLEY CONGREGATION 2006 AT KINGDOM HALL AFTER VIST TO LONDON MUSEUM.

With Maurice for the Convention at Seville,Spain, 2003.

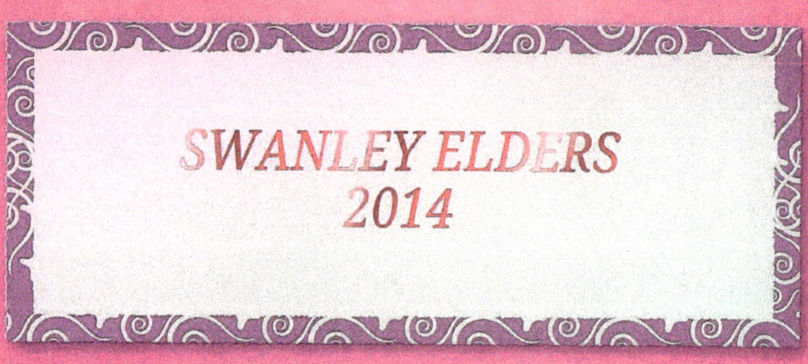
SWANLEY ELDERS
2014

2007

2016 July
Maurice and Vicky
Brighton Convention.

The Grandkids
2017

JULIE TONY
&
HARRY 2017

Graham, sister Pearl,
Vicky, John,
Gordon & Maurice.

**Maria, Jack, Owen,
Lauren, & Adrian
2017**

LOUISA, RICKY, BUDDY
JASPER & GRACIE 2017

With the Family
2017

10 year old Grandson
Owen victorian london
chimney sweep boy.
2017

A year ago, I really thought after more than two years' input the book was about finished, but no, surprise surprise, with my three sisters in mind I found myself writing about the seaside town of Leysdown. However, just prior to that I had passed my book onto a very good friend, Doug Hughes, to see what he thought. Doug had spent all his working life in the publishing world of books and magazines, and I just felt his opinion, and any advice would be priceless. He had had the book for a while, and I felt absolutely delighted when he gave both thumbs up, and said how much he had enjoyed reading the book. However, he did say after a week or two, 'You know, David, you will have to write a sequel to your book. Your grandchildren will want to know what happened next and how your business turned out.' I thanked Doug for his kind words and advice, and reminded him of what was said in the book's introduction, that it would range a specific time period of 20 years, from around the late 1940s until the late 1960s...as a child, teenager and youth. 'Yes, of course,' he said, 'but, David, I really enjoyed reading your book...'

We lost our lovely Doug this year, 2017, a few months ago, aged 89. A man well loved by his family and many friends. I must add, Doug had already lost his wonderful wife, Olive, who died some 10 months earlier. A lovely kind couple, hardly ever apart from each other, always ready to help others. Doug's health had been failing him for some time and knew it was just a matter of time before he joined her in sleep...

In memory of Doug I would like to add in the book a short piece about him and dedicate it to his memory, and also later a short sequel regarding my business to date.

To celebrate the life of

Douglas Edward Hughes

10th March 1928 - 25th April 2017

In memory of Doug Hughes...

Doug was a London boy, born and bred, one of four brothers. He left school around 14 years of age, during the middle of the Second World War.

As regards a job, he began a career in the publishing world of print, starting off as an office boy... interrupted in 1946 by his two years' national service in the army, serving mainly in Germany and Berlin. It was at the time when the famous Second World War trials were taking place. Once demobbed from the army Doug returned to South London and continued his career in the publishing world, later it would involve travel around Europe and staying in hotels from time to time. He retired from his work around the age of 65... At around this time he showed an interest in the Bible and the faith his wife Olive was following...becoming a Christian witness of Jehovah, after her studying and getting baptised in the faith.

For Doug, it would be a steady pace. He would become interested in the faith and the true message of the Bible for himself, in his own time...

However, what would really spur him on was to suffer the loss of his daughter Glenda, at just 42 years of age...Doug would learn and appreciate the promised resurrection of billions of people ...and the opportunity for them to live on a paradise earth, which was always God's original purpose for men and woman. He wanted to see and meet his beloved daughter Glenda again.

Eventually Doug was baptised, along with his wife Olive, and so become an active member of Swanley congregation…

The singing chimney sweep
Tom(my dad)
1967

The chimney sweeping legacy…

Dad's early days of chimney sweeping would have its beginnings in Hoxton, the very heart of the East End of London. A thriving chimney sweep business that went back many generations into the Victorian and Dickens era. It was run by the Brooks family on my Dad's mother's side... Violet Brooks… and if it was possible to be a cockney snob, Nan came close as a candidate, when she spoke of the Brooks family she belonged to.

"They had their own office, yer know," she would say, "where customers would go to book up their chimneys to be swept...also a large yard for handcarts and equipment to be stored, and sacks of soot to be collected and sold on. And also… they were not just your normal sweeps," she would remind me. "They were yer City sweeps, the toffs up there would only have the best in their ouses, yer know, David…" Nan loved to tell me stories of the part of London, the East End where all the family lived. One of her favourites was to remind me that she was born in the same street in Hoxton where the famous music hall singing star Marie Lloyd lived … "yer know".

In 1953 Dad would begin his chimney sweeping career. The business was passed on like a baton, and, with the blessing from the Brooks family, chimney sweeping would have its start locally around Swanley then spread into north Kent and south London, especially so, once I got started in 1970… and of course even more so once my two sons, Tony and Ricky, came on board. However, to start with, Dad would struggle …he had the basic equipment but no knowledge of its use and experience of sweeping. On top of that no work vehicle. He was a young man with no money, no experience, only lots of passion to get started with his business venture, be his own boss. He was impatient to get started… soon he would have just enough money to buy an old 1930s Austin 7 ex-Post Office van, a funny little motor even by 1950s' standards. The bodywork was half wooden, and the footwell was likely to leak when going through a puddle.

The brakes, being on a cable system, would be forever squeaking when his foot applied a little pressure, and he would then receive some funny looks from people passing by... or worse if he were on the inside of a bus full up with passengers, which always seemed the 1950s fashion …and then approaching traffic lights… Dad would learn by just dabbing his foot lightly, eased the squeak. However, if he ever had to hit the brakes hard. The squeak would turn into a rather large screech sound. He would then hope that any large lorry nearby would receive the blame, but more often than not a bus full of people would not be fooled and they would be smiling, even laughing, at the funny little van...as it would pull away in a puff of smoke…

Of course, by then Dad would have passed his driving test… However, that would take a little time, so as a temporary measure, he somehow acquired a sit up and beg type bike with a side wheel, and narrow metal frame to house a long box, just big enough to carry some equipment compliant with chimney sweeping… rods, brushes, hand shovel, various size cloths, and just enough room for half a sack of soot. What a contraption... how Dad hated it, and think of it as a flying bedstead. He discovered that pumping his legs up and down at 30mph the thing would perhaps move at 5 mph, perhaps even 10 mph … downhill...with the wind behind him…

However, if it was an uphill challenge, forget it, jump off and start pushing, like it was an old London hand cart.

Dad's Battle of Waterloo with the bike would happen one wet rainy day outside a café along London Road, close to the Bull of Birchwood.

The rain by then was coming down like stair rods, as he approached the all glass front café, and all Dad could see in his mind's eye was a crowd of sensible people out of the pouring rain drinking hot cups of tea, thinking of the poor souls out in the rotten weather...funny that, Dad at the same was thinking of them, and the crowd of eyes bearing down on him… Roll up, roll up, it's carnival time, let's watch the sweep go by in the pouring rain, on his bedstead flying machine …Yet worse was to come…

What with the pouring rain and thoughts of a café audience, Dad's head may have been down a little extra, and he never saw the parked motor outside the café, so flash bang wallop (what a picture) Dad would crumple off the back of the parked motor onto the wet road accompanied by half a sack of soot and array of cane rods.

Sensing, perhaps laughter coming, from the café, he quickly scooped up the loose equipment, grabbed hold of the bike, snaked it around the parked motor, jumped on it and away into the driving rain… feeling somewhat embarrassed, and humiliated was this once proud 19-year-old paratrooper of the...6th.Airborne, 1944... And part of the war time D-Day campaign, all less than 10 years previously.

When he got home and told Mum the story. He would round it all off in a Tony Hancock type way …saying…OH HOW I HATE MY LIFE, LOOK WHAT IT'S COME DOWN TO...SWEEPING CHIMNEYS IS BAD ENOUGH…BUT… WITH A FLYING BEDSTEAD????....I ASK YA…

Dad would feel a little embarrassed and annoyed over the incident but who cares, the luxury little 1930s ex-Post Office van would soon become the flagship and start of White's chimney sweeping Empire.

Freddie the little gypsy boy and the black hole of soot

Two doors up from where we lived at Lime Road, and next door to my pal Dave Miller, lived a gypsy family...the Yeildings. They were a lovely family, always polite, obliging, and kind – if they had a little surplus produce over from their allotment they would come round and hand some over to my mum.

They were a large family; I don't remember any husband, but it was Mrs Yeilding who ruled the roost, very tiny and slim, and less than 5-feet tall, who did not seem to have any teeth, black hair done up at the back with one plait. To myself, as a 10-year-old, she would seem ancient, but I suppose she would have been aged around 50 years and we would refer to her as Granny Yielding...I somewhat have to try and remember hard the exact number in the family and all their names but I believe it was two brothers Billy and Joey, two sons, one Henry, but the other name escapes me, then a daughter, Mary, who had a small son Freddie, Granny Yielding's grandson, and he was around five years old, having a large mop of brown curly hair, chirpy and a little cheeky, and no doubt a bit spoilt by all the adult attention. One other person I must add of course is Granny Yielding's sister Emily. Now Emily fascinated me because she never spoke, Granny did all the talking for her, while giving her various instructions to carry out, which she did without a word. Though short, Emily was not slim but rather on the stout side, hair fashion the same as Granny, with a black plait.

She would remind me of an Indian squaw… that is just how I would think of the family at the time, as Indians coming in off the plains, onto the reservation and so learn…White man ways. And they did, both grannies' sons became well educated, and went on to have good careers. And as for Freddie, Mary was very young when she had him (another story). However, it was Granny Yeilding who would take charge of him. Freddie was very bright, and Granny knew his worth and would visit the local school from time to time, especially if she thought he was being unfairly overlooked.

On a final note about the Yeilding family I will end with two funny stories.

1.. THE HORSE..

My pal next door, Dave Miller, told me this story, as it all happened a few years before we moved to Lime Road.

Once the Yeilding family acquired a council house in Lime Road, their travelling life was finished with...However, they could not part with their beloved horse, well not straight away…so they brought the horse with them for a while, until they found a good home for him and so be cared for. No doubt the horse would have been tethered with a length of rope in the back-garden enclosure.

The problem I had at the time was only hearing part of the story, so therefore just as youngsters are prone to do, one's imagination would kick in. My pal David may have just been a baby or infant at the time they moved next door to him, and so not aware of all the facts himself...And so David just said to me, "When the Yeildings moved in next door to live, they brought their horse with them…"

So that gave me the giggles to start with, as all I could imagine is the horse living in the house with a crowd of people…but then we were both off, and thinking the sort of things a horse might like to do indoors …e.g. On a cold day in front of the fire he might like to lie on the settee with crossed hoofs….on days when he got a little bored, someone might open the window so he could stick his head out and watch the world go by…at night he would be useful: you could jump on his back, and then he would take you up the stairs to your bedroom…

Freddie's great escape...(almost)

Our back garden was like a tiny meadow, the grass laid down flat in a kind of distressed, given up look. No wonder – it would never see a lawn mower or a fork to turn the soil. Some of the back gardens of neighbours you could look along, and notice crops being grown and cared for, potatoes, peas, runner beans and so on...but not so with Dad, growing crops and marigold flowers was not for him, but for the flat cap, slippers and pipe smoking brigade, or so he thought.

His fingers were of the black variety not green. As for pipe dreams, while pushing rods and brushes through chimney pots his thoughts would be more of singing, and music.

Though a fork and spade would not be seen around the garden, yet nevertheless, one day a spade would come in great use. My pal Dave and I decided, wouldn't it be a good idea to dig a 5-foot-deep hole in the garden, near the back of the shed, up a little, and close to the chain link fence, so be a little out of the way; then once the hole was dug we would dig out the side as a cave like camp, with the roof being about 1-foot thick. We cracked on. Like two mini moles, all day, and as it was the busy chimney sweeping season, autumn time, Dad would likely be working a long day; in fact we had just about finished when I heard the van pull up. By then we were sitting in our underground camp, we had found some old cloths to sit on, as it had been a long hard day. While resting we discussed what improvements we could make to our underground apartment, as we both felt so proud of our long day's effort and looked forward to doing any additional refinements.

Dad had now arrived back from work, and we could hear him walking over so we climbed out of the hole. The reception we received was most unexpected, but very sudden; perhaps, he too had had a hard day and was also tired...Not a word was said, but what I do well remember, was him taking three long strides jumping up in the air two-foot, and bringing down his full 14 stone weight crashing through the camp roof.

A day's hard work destroyed in a matter of seconds...I felt shocked and upset at the time ...Dad, he just turned around walked down the garden and went indoors, still without saying a word – that would come at another time…Of course he'd done the only right thing, to us two young lads we did not realise the danger we were in, if the roof was to collapse while we were inside...The next main decision was to tidy up the hole type ditch in the garden. However, the busy sweeping season was underway, so Dad decided, in his wisdom, to leave it a few months until springtime, then he would sort it out; after all, no one goes near that area in the wintertime, do they?

In the meantime there would be some sacks of surplus soot and I do mean soot, the real McCoy. In the 1950s before smokeless zones, house after house would burn household coal, and the soot, well you would leave it at the address or lose it, as best way you could. Dad could be artful rather than devious, if a person did not mind their soot being left somewhere on the garden they may have received the last customer's soot and the vacuum being emptied as well. However, surplus soot would find its way into a sack or container, and be carried along in the van. That said, it would all have to be disposed of somehow, some time, and the sooner the better, as room in the motor would be limited, so, for a few weeks the 5-foot hole in the garden would do just nicely, and so gradually be filled with the best graded house coal soot… Then, Dad decided he would then throw soil across the hole full of soot area come the springtime in just a few months …After all, he thought, no one goes near that area in the wintertime, do they?

Bonfire night

I would love bonfire night during November time, and the two or three week build up to the event, small groups of boys could be seen everywhere, dragging along tree branches, old furniture, anything burnable and not nailed down. And of course the main event, the fireworks that were readily available in local shops... for myself like many young boys all I was only interested in were bangers and rockets. There was only one time I tried something different; it was when I decided for a change, with my savings, to buy a box of mixed fireworks: rockets, Catherine wheels, jumping jacks, and so on. However, a spark from the bonfire went into the box and the whole lot went up in one go… A big lesson I learned that night, in future go back to buying just bangers and rockets again.

On this night, in the 1950s the bonfire was lit and as usual we had the family gathering, as well as a few friends and neighbours such as little Freddie, buzzing all over the place. After a while everything would be coming to its end, even the King Edward baked potatoes were being raked out of the glowing embers of the fire to be eaten. I don't remember any kitchen foil being wrapped round potatoes in those days. To demonstrate a King Edward's potato's worthiness of being eaten, a must was to have a thick black-charred skin around the potato; the prize would then be received, but only after first removing the thick black charred skin, and, then, most important, all this to be done with half burned fingers. One would then retrieve their sacred reward, the potato itself, likely, the size of a large marble…

Normally once the main event of fireworks was over the sparklers would come out…so did Freddie – if anyone was going to steal the final scene for the evening's end of events it was going to be him, and if anyone could best tell the story it would be my Dad, in this way.

Freddie the little gypsy boy with a mop of brown curly hair was given a sparkler to hold. He got so excited, he started off holding up the sparkler and running backwards, forwards, all over the place and noisy with it…WOOOOOOOO WOOOOOOO. Still holding up the sparkler, he started running around in circles and moving further down the garden, WOOOOO WOOOOOO. By now he was almost out of sight down the dark far end of the garden, towards the back of the shed. Dad at this point of telling the story would suddenly pause, and clap his hands just once, saying, "Freddie's gone, the sparkler's gone…no hold on, hold on... I think I see movement and, yes, a small puff of soot down the end of the garden…" Freddie had found, dived, and submerged himself head first into the 5-foot black hole of soot; quickly he resurfaced and did not stop running till he got home to his granny two doors up the road…

At this stage no one could stop laughing at what they had just seen. As for Dad he expressed a big guilty grin, and, a few of the others were heard saying poor little Freddie, hope he's okay…I expect his granny will sort him out.

Fifteen minutes went by and things were starting to quieten down, just a few stifled laughs over what they had seen. Suddenly down the end of the garden, near the back door there appeared a tiny figure... It was Granny Yeilding calling up the garden to my dad: "TOM, TOM, WHAT HAVE YOU DONE TO MY FREDDIE? HE CAME HOME COVERED IN SOOT FROM TOP TO TOE. I HAVE STRIPPED OFF ALL HIS CLOTHES, PUT HIM IN THE BATH AND HAVE TAKEN HIM UP TO HIS BED." Dad reacted as quick as he could, with innocent surprise and all the charm he could muster… "Oh Granny, what can I say, there was a pile of soot, I did warn the children to keep away, I'm really sorry about poor little Freddie, but I mean, nobody goes near that area in the winter, do they?… poor Freddie, bless him."

Review …sequel … and conclusion

As I was writing some of the stories that had happened during the 50s and 60s I realised how funny the times were... as a child it would all seem very normal though. On a good day sweeping, Dad would come through the back doorway, with a sooty face and black hands and would empty his pockets on the table in the middle of the room of what always seemed to be loads of silver coins, and some 10 bob notes and pound notes. I don't ever remember him having a wallet or some kind of bag, to hold the money; it was just his pockets.

Mum would hover in the background ready to descend on the day's takings and sort out the needs for the weekly budget, while putting money away for monthly outlays, even considering funds for the rest of the year as need be. Mum proved an excellent manager over the many years; Dad knew it best to leave all the financial management to her to deal with so it would free him to focus on other things, like a good bath, clean clothes, and a cup of tea. The house would always seem clean and tidy, especially difficult when you consider the nature of the job Dad was doing… Somehow a line was drawn outside the back door with an invisible notice that read WARNING NO SOOT SHALL CROSS THIS LINE…I just don't remember seeing signs of soot around the house. I think they both worked hard at keeping any loose soot on the right side of the line…Dad would take off his boots, strip down to his vest and in the kitchen sink spend 5 minutes scrubbing up his hands and arms up to the elbows like the true chimney surgeon that he was; in the meantime Mum would be running the bath water.

They worked hard knowing how easy it would be to allow loose soot to have a free hand travelling around the house on furniture, the floor, and clothing. It was an obvious daily hazard of the job.

If you were to discuss this topic with my mum it would perhaps prompt her to tell a very funny story that would bring tears to her eyes. Up to and around the 1940s neat graded soot had a value for farmland, small holdings, allotments, and gardens etc…

The London soot salesman

This story was told to my mum back in the 1960s.

One day a fairly elderly gentleman knocked on the front door to book a chimney to be swept. After the business transaction was done he went on to say that he was a soot salesman during the 1930s. He would travel around London collecting sacks of soot, which would have value, and be used on farms, allotments and gardens etc. He would call on certain pre-arranged days at various addresses of chimney sweeps…At one address he went to, it was a sweep's house with a large family of about eight children whose ages were from about three years up to about 13 years old… Some sacks of soot would be stored in part of the house, because of lack of storage space. When he called on the arranged day for collection suddenly all the children would appear from behind the door and elsewhere, all with sooty faces. Mum laughed lots when told, and so did Dad when she later told him the story. Afterwards Mum could hardly repeat telling the story to anyone because it would make her laugh so much.

While talking of booking work at the door, that did not happen so often as booking work on the telephone, which was positioned in a mini office area by the front door... It would mean wherever you were in the house you could hear the telephone going off and the business transaction taking place. By then we had moved from Lime Road to Cherry Avenue…a lovely house, much bigger and on a corner plot of land.

Dad soon had a garage erected. I don't remember it being used for motors but it was excellent for storage.

As for the office in the hallway, like with so many small family businesses, a telephone for business would also double up for family use as well, so when the phone rang and you answered it chances are it may be someone who wanted a chimney swept. Business and private calls seemed all mixed together, but then, during the mid-1960s many homes still did not have a landline and people would have to use public phone boxes nearby, so we considered ourselves fortunate.

Dad could be hilariously funny at times, and Mum would be in bits trying hard to stay in control, especially if she was on the phone dealing with a customer, and Dad was making her laugh.

It would start off by perhaps Mum putting her hand over the mouthpiece and calling down the hallway to Dad sitting in the back room. It would go something like this… "Tom, I know you have a busy day Friday but you're working at the Tree estate Dartford and this customer at Willow Road on the Tree estate is just round the corner – do you mind if I book it in?" Mum did not like the thought of Dad over working, but then the prospect of a little extra cash was sometimes too tempting. She would still have her hand over the mouthpiece waiting for Dad's reply, and, many a time out of sight, his answer would be to bray like a donkey being harnessed ready for work…E..ORE …E..ORE…E.ORE, then make the sound with his shoes like the scraping of hooves on the stable floor. Mum would accept that as a reluctant yes, and as a true professional in control, book in the job, at the same time controlling the laughter, as Dad in the background would continue being funny knowing he had her on the ropes.

Also what was funny, especially looking back on it all, mainly the 1950s and up to the mid-1960s, was how the snob in Dad would rear its head –unlike his mum, our nan, who was proud of her roots, and satisfied with her station in life; perhaps if she was a snob it was for being a London cockney.

Dad in many ways would often remind me of the character, and also slightly in looks too, of Harold Steptoe. It was the famous comedy series Steptoe and Son, which is still shown on TV. Harold could never escape his roots as a rag and bone man. If ever he got near to it, his dad would make sure he ruined things, reined him back in, and for a while kill off the snob in him. Harold just wanted to improve his life but it seemed impossible. Both Harold and Tom, my dad, felt denied of the better things in life, and why not? But the irony was not being able to shake off their roots, Harold being a cockney rag and bone man, and my dad a cockney chimney sweep.

Dad's resentment of the poor hand of cards dealt to him, may have been from after the war years, coming back home from army life and then to support a young family with no money, and work that offered little prospects and poor wages. But the biggest blow Dad felt was his lack of education; it would have a profound effect on his reading and writing. At a later stage, I would hear Dad relate how spending so much time with his mum during the 1930s summer months, on the farms of Kent fruit picking, then hop picking, caused him to get behind on his education, and what with starting work in London at just 13, his lack of education would have to stay on hold, and of course once the 1940s and Second World War got underway, Hitler would not wait for Dad to catch up on his schooling. During the 1930s Dad though would forget to tell of the fun, freedom, and lack of schooling he would have enjoyed with a few other London boys on the fruit and hop fields of Kent... His lack of education seemed to really kick in when he told me of the time he was trying to compose and write a letter while in the regimental barracks, and among other lads milling around, he would ask how do you spell this word, how do you spell that word and so on; this all set up barrack room bantering among the lads especially when Dad asked, "How do you spell church?" It would set off an inferiority complex that would only right itself at evening school classes after the war years. Dad would then catch up on his lack of education then, something that he also dearly wanted for his own children starting with my sister Fay in 1950, and myself a year later.

In time my sisters would all do well, starting with Fay who was school girl gold. I have spoken earlier in the book about Fay and all I need add is at 15 years old she would spend three years at Erith College for hairdressing. My other sisters became S.R.N nurses and midwives, and one of them, Marion, even qualified to be a school teacher as well in the 1970s but chose a nursing career which she still pursues.

As for my own academic skills, hang on a minute I believe I've written them down on the back of a postage stamp somewhere… however, I would like to say, though not the best of students, or sharpest tool in the box, I remain grateful to the state school system, over the 10 years, it taught me a basic education; the rest of my education would come through life itself and the responsibility of your freedom of choice…in other words I was not going to be a rocket scientist (sorry, Dad)... more likely a chimney sweep (sorry again).

I believe that being a half decent boxer in my teenage years may have softened Dad a little and made some small amends. Anyway, by then he realised I was not going to be a rocket scientist after all.

After various jobs from the age of 15, then from the age of 22 I started up my own cleaning business, so it would be a couple of years before the chimney sweeping would have its start... and I was not surprised I took to sweeping. As a school boy just before leaving school I would go out and help Dad on a Saturday morning until early afternoon; I would earn a 10 bob note (50 pence) pocket money. Dad would always be singing as we drove along... even when working around people's homes he would sing if he could get away with it. Though I was in my early teens, I knew somehow one day I would enjoy doing the chimney sweep job for a living.

It would be the same with both my sons Tony and Ricky. I would never coax them into doing the job, but they knew it's what they wanted to do. My dad would also not coax or encourage; in fact one day Ricky had to pop into my dad's house for some reason while on the way home from school. While there his grandad said to him, "Well Ricky, what is it you want to do when you leave school?" "I want to be a chimney sweep like my dad," he then said. Dad's face would drop, and he said to Ricky, "Now what do you want to do that for…" Ricky almost 30 years later still remembers my dad saying those words, and laughs; in the meantime he's earned a good living, has a nice home…lovely family.

Both Ricky and Tony have always been very hard workers. The nature of the work has changed, especially since my dad's generation 60 years ago, and my generation from 40 years ago.

My dad would leave a foundation for me to build on, which meant ladderwork, and getting on to roofs, and so be involved in fitting pots and cowls, also construction work, building, and sometimes removing chimney stacks, which often involved scaffolding, then repointing, repair, lead flashing, and it could often lead to roof work from time to time... such as replacing roof tiles, another part of our work these days. So the bar would be raised in my day and further still when Tony and Ricky came on board as we then began fitting wood burning stoves, and fireplaces.

That side of things has been carried well forward by the boys – we even have a small shop in West Malling named "the little stove shop" and managed by Tony's wife Julie. Just as I was keen to make a go at the construction side of the chimney sweep business (whereas my dad who was going into his fifties showed little interest) I too when going into my fifties, had not the same passion and interest in stove fitting – it can be a very complex and demanding side of things catering for the many varied needs of customers, and do a good job and please them, all at the same time. I have to say the boys do very well overall and seem well liked by the customers.

For myself, now I am going into my 70s, I may go out with Ricky just in a fetch and carry role, but I seldom go out, and to be honest, though it's taken the best part of 10 years to accept and not mind having to be so involved, when I do go out to give a hand I then realise just how physically hard and tough a job it is...30 years ago when I was the same age, I would be doing the job on my own, but then it would have been mainly chimney sweeping and some amount of ladder work; these days it is more diverse and two are often required. Before Tony first came along to work with me I spent 13 years working by myself. It took a while to get used to it, working with someone, even my own son.

Eventually, over time, Tony would become very adaptable and took to the job in a natural type of way. Once Ricky came on board they then would work well together after a few years...

Ricky and Tony, it would be true to say, are the main force driving the business along these days, like they're in the driving seat. I only go out if needed on rare occasions, more happy to take charge of daily deliveries, and keeping sheds and areas tidy. I have even developed a limp in recent years to go with my new job role.

Tony and Ricky are both into their early forties now, my age when they first started working with me, around 25 years ago, quarter of a century. Just amazing how quickly the time has gone.

Both boys have done well, the way they seem to deal with everything, even when it seems thrown at them, and they take it on the chin without a fuss. I am very proud of them both, and all they do.

Ricky... it was like he would always know exactly what it was he would want to do with his life, from the age of a young teenager, and it was not as if myself and his mum would talk, or be forever trying to steer him in the right direction. True it may be nice to receive a little of the credit, but it would only be in as much as Ricky may have recognised what an important part our faith would play in our family lives. Looking back, I wonder if I could or should have done a lot more, but fortunately, it seems Ricky could not have turned out any better than he has…He would call locally at people's homes to talk about God's Kingdom, and a new world. In time he would also be baptised in the J.W. faith and become a ministerial servant in his early 20s and a young elder helping the local congregation at Dartford before the age of 30...

For many years he gave public talks, and still does. And he may have a part on a convention programme from time to time, but he still finds time for the family and recreation with his children…

He could have achieved anything he wanted to do in life, he seems a natural leader (unlike his dad), so having a high-flying career, profession. He's into watching different sports and was a very good football player, and is a season ticket holder at Charlton F.C. Perhaps, just maybe, he could have once played for them instead.

But then I know his present life is much more important to him.

This story I have just told has not been said before. If Ricky ever reads the story while I'm still around it will perhaps make him smile for about

10 seconds, then he'll start to talk about other thing on his mind – that's how sentimental he is…I am now trying hard at this moment to round off the story as best as I can. People may say, it sounds like you're quite proud of your son Ricky – the short answer would be "yes I suppose I am". But then short answers I am not known for…but rather, perhaps, sentimental answers, just a little... perhaps.

And the word sentimental is often how a person may view the chimney sweep…whatever the equipment you use such as power brushes and other power tools for cleaning or unblocking chimneys.

They may still think of Mary Poppins or Charles Dickens and Victorian London – it does not matter to what degree of sophistication you think the job level has reached, it's still viewed as a humble occupation by the general public. At least, though, you're not the undertaker; people are much more likely to smile or laugh when it's you that turns up...and I too think it's quite funny at times when people accept you into their lovely homes, a sooty face, and perhaps even make you a cup of tea.

Recently Ricky asked if I wanted to go and work with him for the day. It was mainly a day of sweeping chimneys, then at the end of the day I sat in the van finishing off writing out a chimney sweeping certificate and receipt to give Ricky for the customer. Now, Ricky even in jeans and casual clothes would still be clean cut; evenings and weekends you will find him right dapper in a smart suit and tie.

For now, it's just a moment in time but I look at Ricky who is close up to the van with a very sooty face, and I remembered what he said all those years ago, when asked what he wanted to do when he left school – "I want to be a chimney sweep like my dad." So the London chimney sweep legacy lives on, our cockney nan would be so proud, and also, in case I've forgotten to mention it, the street in Hoxton, London, where Nan was born, was where the famous music hall star Marie Lloyd lived…yer know.

And the final sequel

During the summer of 2017, a young chap named Will Noble contacted us with regard to him writing up a story to feature in the internet-based magazine named the LONDONIST… Will was a journalist and editor of the magazine which includes interesting stories of people doing unusual jobs, or activities in and around London. He thought we may have a story to tell about chimney sweeping, and our London heritage and connection that may be of interest.

"Will" would travel down from London by train, would stay for about an hour asking us questions …to get the full story and put it on the Londonist site…

By Will Noble

Will Noble London Still Has Chimney Sweeps ... We Met Three Of Them

"I think when you're growing up in your teens, you don't want to say you dad's a chimney sweep. But when you start going to work, and people say 'what do you do?' you say 'guess'. And they never guess what you do. And when you say 'chimney sweep', they're like 'I didn't know that existed!'".

David White (centre) and his sons Tony (left) and Ricky

Ricky White always wanted to be a sweep. There's more than a hint ofthis in the picture he drew, aged 11, of his father-proudly titled "My dad". "You really only become a chimney sweep because it's in the family," says Ricky.

"It's not like you go to the career office, and come out a sweep," chips in Tony White, Ricky's older brother. The two are sat with their dad, David, in his surprisingly immaculate living room in Swanley (only later do we clock the black soot smudges around the door frames). All three work for Whites Chimney and Stoves, between them, covering much of south east London, Kent and parts of Surrey. Theirs may be a profession that peaked in Victorian London, but it lives on -and is now enjoying a semi-rebirth, as woodburners and fireplaces become de rigueur once more.

The picture Ricky drew of his dad, aged 11

Whites has been going since 1953, when David's dad Tom ("a cross between Tony Hancock and Harold Steptoe, a snob at heart, but a lovable one") accepted his true calling. "He had a good voice," says David, "always singing while he was working."

"For about six years he went into opera. And did piano playing. He was a frustrated musician. And frustrated singer. And frustrated chimney sweep!"

But soot's been in the family blood longer than that; David's grandmother's side of the family-the Brooks -swept too. Her father, Tom Brooks may have sported a blackened face and hands, but he had a pure enough soul. He was a vestryman, not to mention a mouthpiece for the temperance movement in his native East End. So respected was Brooks in his day, he became Mayor of Bethnal Green in 1931.

David has been sweeping since 1970

There is a striking picture of Brooks as he walks the streets of the East End -his cap, face -even teeth coloured in with soot; his back bearing a bundle of rods; a gaggle of flat-capped onlookers gazing upon him like he's some deity. Mayor of Bethnal Green he may have been, but Brooks never hung up the brushes. Indeed, the story goes that he was invited to a tea party at Buckingham Palace in his capacity as mayor, and still fulfilled his sweeping duties that morning. "I don't know if he turned up at the palace looking like a sweep!" laughs Tony.

Brooks was apparently responsible for moving Brick Lane's Sunday market from the northern end -something that didn't go down well with all the locals. If it hadn't been for who Brooks was, Tony suggests, he'd have been beaten up.

"The villains, the gangs-they all respected him," says Tony, "He wasn't frightened of them. He'd sit outside his house on a Sunday, and people would come up to him and debate things with him."

While Tom Brooks probably swept 10 chimneys or so a day on the same road, Whites cast the net much further. "We've got vans, whereas he would have walked to a house with his rods, cleaned the chimley, walked to the next house round the corner," says Tony. ("Chimley" and "chimney" are interchangeable in the family's parlance, although when we point this out, they say they've never noticed).

My Grandad encouraged his son Tom (my father) to go into the sweeping profession during the 1950's post war period. Grandad would travel up to the East End of London, to connect with the Brooks Family. He would meet family members and then bring back some sweeping equipment. It was like the baton of acceptance was handed over from the Brooks to the Whites. Grandad also located a firm that he knew of, who specialised in sweeping equipment, while he was there. This company was just about to close down, however, they said that from records, they had been trading with the Brooks Family for many generations, dating back over 200 years.

But has anything in the nature of the actual sweeping changed?

"Sweeping has always been rods and brushes", says Tony, "but the equipment's got better". The modern, tough plastic brushes (David keeps an old horsehair brush for nostalgia's sake, and sometimes lends it out to kids for school fancy dress) are fitted to a power drill – so you can clean at a zippier rate. A vacuum also helps stop soot and dust escape around the room.

The old horsehair brush that David keeps for nostalgia's sake. David remembers the days when you would send kids out onto the street to watch the chimney, and shout when they saw the brush poke out of the top.

That doesn't stop customers being paranoid; "Sometimes you're filthy dirty and you stink of soot," says Tony, "and you turn up in someone's house and they may say to you straight away 'are you going to make a mess?'"

"Tom may have come along and made a load of mess. Where as nowadays, we can't get away with it. You're expected to keep the soot and dust contained."

So in all their years on the job they've never created a Laurel and Hardy-style scene? "Out of the hundreds and thousands of chimneys, you're going to get one or two that are a disaster," admits Tony, "You never know till you clean a chimney, how bad it's going to be."

This prompts David to remember a job in Sutton years ago, where the vacuum bag had been perforated. "Tony didn't know it was happening," laughs David. "The bloke, he had a temper. He'd gone out, left us to it-he come in the room, and he just went like that [mimics touching dust with fingers] ... and then he went bananas. He said 'I hope you're insured.'"

"He was so angry, he walked down the garden to cool off and I thought 'that's just what we need' and we went bananas with the hand brushes, all round the room. And in 10 minutes, it was amazing what we done. I was panicking at the same time though."

Archaic traditions must keep up with the times. But as chimney sweeps, they still get covered in soot? "Only on a good day, yeah," says Tony, "If you come home clean, your wife will say 'why are you clean?'"

While sweeping may be the bread and butter of the business, each generation has branched out, adding news skills to the portfolio. The proliferation of gas boilers in the 1970s triggered a steep decline in real fireplaces, yet rising gas and oil prices have since put wood burning stoves back in the picture. Of course, these, and open fires, are back in vogue too. "The difference with our life now," says Tony, "is we have something because we want it. Whereas they had it because they needed it -they had no central heating."

"You had to have a coal fire, otherwise there was no heating. These days it's a luxury, there's a romantic side."

Ironically, Whites also specialise in the structural job of taking chimneys out. Not everybody needs them. "However," says David, "we often reinstate chimneys back to how they were before they were taken out perhaps 30 or 40 years previous. Or, from time to time we actually build a chimney or install a flue system, normally on the outside of a house, if we are fitting a stove or fireplace if the house has not been built with a chimney flue."

The act of sending young boys up the chimneys might have long been banished-but both Tony and Ricky know a couple of lads they hope will continue their business.

"My son, Harry, is leaving school next week," says Tony, "and my brother's got a son leaving in about six years time. They're the next generation. My boy's strong and doesn't mind getting his hands dirty. You're either that way or you're not."

Whites, it would seem, are always that way.

Harry age 16

Harry, the new generation

“Whites” chimney sweep code... and rule 1...

Rule 1 code...

“Never trust a chimney sweep with a clean face and wearing a white shirt”.

My 16 year old grandson Harry is certainly a quick learner, through only five months working with us he learned the “rule 1 code” in no time at all. I just know he’s going high places in the business, already he’s climbing up onto roofs and chimney stacks, fitting chimney pots and cowls with his Dad Tony. However on a more serious note, and joking aside I would just like to say what a lovely kid Harry is, a right little gem. He attends college 3 days a week learning building skills, a three year course. It means spending 2 days a week with our business and longer when the college is closed. Harry like Tony is a natural hard worker keen to learn, helpful, considerate, very well liked by family, friends and the customers.

“ IT`S TO YOU,IF WE BELONG”

**GOLD,LIKE DEW ALWAYS THERE BUT MAY BE GONE,
BUT NOT TO YOU IF WE BELONG.
FIFTY YEARS SO QUICKLY DONE,FIFTY MORE WILL FOLLOW ON,
YET THE KINGDOM HOPE AND OUR FAITH, STILL WE BELONG.**

**A KINGDOM TO BLESS ALL,PEACE,GOOD HEALTH,EVEN YOUTH
OUR GOD WILL RENEW,AND THOSE ASLEEP WILL RISE AND JOIN
US TOO IN A WORLD OF HOPE FOR ALL NOT JUST THE FEW...
SO GIVE PRAISE TO GOD FOR ALL HE HAS DONE,
FOR IT`S TO YOU IF WE BELONG...**

2017

Thank you for taking time to look through the book.

Remember...

"Never trust a chimney sweep with a clean face and wearing a white shirt".

Regards, David.

With Tony & Ricky
2017

Before you go
if you feel the book a worthwhile read we would appreciate & be so gratefull if you would consider leaving a short review at Amazon books.

Thankyou.

www.ingramcontent.com/pod-product-compliance
Ingram Content Group UK Ltd.
Pitfield, Milton Keynes, MK11 3LW, UK
UKHW062307290726
14090UKWH00018B/928